NATIONAL STATUARY HALL

in the Nation's Capitol

NATIONAL STATUARY
HALL *in the Nation's Capitol*

By
MYRTLE CHENEY MURDOCK
Doctor of Education

*The history of the world is but
the biography of great men.*

THOMAS CARLYLE

MONUMENTAL PRESS, INC.,
Washington, D. C.
1955

Copyright 1955

By Myrtle Cheney Murdock

Preface

This study of statues in the Capitol Building of the United States is meant to give quick and rather comprehensive information on the bronze and marble statues treasured by the Government of the United States. The overall picture should not only include photographic reproductions of the statues themselves but it certainly should give the reader a thumb-nail biography of each American statesman, scientist, missionary, colonizer, or empire builder, whose statue has been placed with such love and reverence in the Nation's Capitol. Then, too, the book would seem incomplete without a character summing-up of each American pictured here, this statement to be from some other American who has also become nationally known through the years.

As the statue study developed it became evident that the whole story of America is epitomized by this bronze and marble gathering in the Capitol Building. So rewarding is this comprehensive view of American history from the vantage point of National Statuary Hall that a brief story of this great narrative as outlined to the world by these distinguished Americans is the concluding chapter of this book.

Every book published usually brings forth three questions for the author to answer: Why did you do it? Where did you get it? What do you hope from it? Let me answer these questions at once.

As an official Guide in the Capitol Building of the United States I find that our American people actually want the information which I have assembled in this book. They are glad to know that the Congress of the United States converted the second unit of the Capitol Building—the old House of Representatives' Chamber—into a National Statuary Hall with the following legislation:

". . . and the President is authorized to invite all the States to provide and furnish statues, in marble or bronze, not exceeding two in number for each State, of deceased persons who have been citizens thereof, and illustrious for their historic renown or for distinguished civic or military service, such as each State may deem to be worthy of this national commemoration; and when so furnished the same shall be placed in the old Hall of the House of Representatives, in the Capitol of the United States, which is set apart, or so much thereof as may be necessary as a National Statuary Hall."

It was Senator Morrill of Vermont who introduced the Bill into Congress in 1864 converting the old House of Representatives' Chamber into a Hall for statuary, and he did it with these memorable words:

"To what end more useful or grand and at the same time simple and inexpensive, can we devote this Hall than to ordain that it shall be set apart for the reception of such statuary as each State shall elect to be deserving of this lasting commemoration? Will not all the States with generous emulation proudly respond, and thus furnish a new evidence that the Union will clasp and hold forever all its jewels—the glory of the past—civil, military, and judicial, in one hallowed spot where those who will be here to aid in carrying on the Government may daily receive fresh inspiration and new incentives, and where pilgrims from all parts of the Union, as as well as from foreign lands, may come and behold a gallery filled with such American manhood as succeeding generations will delight to honor, and see also the actual form and mold of those who have inerasably fixed their names on the pages of history."

Since it was the thought of Congress in 1864 that two statues from each state could be accommodated in the old House of Representatives' Chamber, everything went smoothly until 1932 when the total number of statues in National Statuary Hall reached 65. After an authorized study of the struc-

7

tural condition of the Hall by a competent engineer, Concurrent Resolution No. 47 was passed by Congress providing for relocation of statues out of the overcrowded Chamber.

In 1934 the actual relocation of statues began. It was decided then that only one statue from each State could safely remain in the old House of Representatives' Chamber, and that all other statues given by the States should be placed in other halls about the Capitol, thus giving us today six additions to National Statuary Hall: The Rotunda; The Senate Connection; The Vestibule South of the Rotunda; The Vestibule Facing the old Supreme Court Chamber; and The Hall of Columns. All of these Halls are on the main floor of the Capitol with the exception of the Hall of Columns which is on the ground floor at the South end of the Building. Thus every statue given by the States is not only legally a part of National Statuary Hall but is so considered by the Congress of the United States regardless of the present location of the statue.

In addition to the present 78 statues given by the States, the Government owns 8 others, acquired either by gift or by commission, five of these occupying cherished positions in the Capitol before any State responded to the 1864 invitation to present statues. In fact, Rhode Island made the first contribution to National Statuary Hall when she sent the marble statue of Nathaniel Greene in 1870.

The bronze statue of Thomas Jefferson, now in the Rotunda, was the gift of Captain Levy in 1834; the marble statue of Thomas Jefferson was acquired by commission in 1855; the marble statue of John Hancock came by commission in 1861; the marble statue of Benjamin Franklin was executed by commission in 1863; the marble statue of Alexander Hamilton, now in the Rotunda, came by commission in 1868; the marble statue of Abraham Lincoln, now in the Rotunda, was acquired by commission in 1871; the marble statue of Edward Dickinson Baker, now in the Rotunda, was voted by Congress in 1873; and the marble statue of General Ulysses S. Grant, now in the Rotunda, was the gift of the Grand Army of the Republic in 1900. Thus we have today in the Capitol Building 86 statues—78 of these being legally a part of National Statuary Hall, and the other 8 being considered temporarily a part of National Statuary Hall by the author for purposes of this study.

And where did I get my information? It has come from the Office of the Architect of the Capitol, from the Library of Congress, and from the Congressional Record. During the 16 years that Mr. Murdock was Congressman from Arizona I had many occasions to thank the Capitol Architect's Office and the Library of Congress for an opportunity to make any search necessary to a project. That situation has not changed.

And most certainly I should mention the invaluable help that Mr. Murdock has been on this project. His broad knowledge of history and government and his almost uncanny acquaintance with these great men of the past, whose lives not only influenced history, but whose lives were influenced by history, give to this book a certain charm of overall accuracy and appreciation for the past which never could have been acquired without him.

Now, what do I hope from this study? I hope that every State will develop new pride in its gift to National Statuary Hall and that the remaining States will soon add their own contribution to this assemblage of America's Great. I hope that schools and parents will use National Statuary Hall as a teaching device—and what noble lessons in character, service, patriotism and sacrifice they will find there. And I hope that the following words of Alexander H. Stephens of Georgia may actually be believed by young America. Said Congressman Stephens—who served in the House of Representatives for 16 years before the War between the States and then served there for 9 years after the War:

"The National Statuary Hall will teach the youth of the land in succeeding generations as they come and go that the chief end of human effort should be usefulness to mankind, and that all true fame which should be perpetuated by public pictures, statues and monuments is to be acquired only by noble deeds and high achievements and the establishment of a character founded upon the principles of truth, uprightness and inflexible integrity."

Introduction

Great nations differ markedly as to how they hold in memory their historic dead. Egypt built her pyramids; Greece her mausoleums; Rome her triumphal arches and the Germanic peoples had both mythical and actual valhallas for their warriors. Coming down the centuries England has her Westminster Abbey; France has her Pantheon; Germany has her Unter Den Linden and Russia has actually embalmed the bodies of Lenin and Stalin and placed them where they may be viewed under glass to be thus the center of a cult. America differs greatly in method and purpose from all these.

In America we have several "halls of fame" in various cities but this book is about those figures in bronze and marble centering in and around Statuary Hall in the Capitol Building in Washington. The clusters of the statues at our national capital, placed mostly in old Statuary Hall proper and several adjacent halls and corridors, all together constitute our National Statuary Hall. Although this assemblage is placed amid historic and impressive surroundings it may be considered less impressive than such in other nations because less magnificent than some of the Old World pantheons. However, our collection in the Capitol does fairly epitomize America's romantic past and portray in bronze and marble the spirit of our history as we view it.

Americans love peace but have been much at war throughout a colorful history and yet the Capitol statuary constitutes more a "Pantheon of Genius" than a valhalla of warriors. Even the soldiers who are there are characterized as "Soldier-statesmen" and most of them are as well remembered for their skill with the pen as with the sword. The only kings in these halls of fame are statesmen with that name rather than men with that title.

To date 78 statues have been furnished by 42 of our States under the Congressional Act of 1864 which set apart the Old House Chamber to receive them after the House of Representatives moved into its new quarters in 1857 when the new House wing was completed. Under the terms and spirit of the Act of 1864 the choice of the individuals to be thus honored was not to lodge at Washington but at the various state capitals as each State was invited to furnish not more than two statues in bronze or marble of that state's most distinguished deceased citizens. Both the choice and the giving were thus left up to the states. The varied types of the persons to be honored is not to be wondered at in view of the varied sections of this vast country, and the varied nature of local history in those different parts.

The Honor Roll is not yet complete, of course, and although the beginning was made nearly one hundred years ago, there is no great hurry to complete it. Other new states are yet to come. In one and two-thirds centuries America has grown from thirteen to forty eight states and spread across this wide continent. From new states yet to be formed, as well as from the six younger states still unrepresented, other distinguished representatives will be sent to this most distinguished Congress of men in bronze and marble at the national capital.

Who are these historic individuals who have been thus elected by their respective states, not now to sit alive in legislative chambers for a term of years, but to stand forever in history in the legislative halls of this greatest legislative Capitol on earth? As has been said, many of them had been soldier-statesmen, but more of them in life had been Members of Congress than had attained high officer rank in military service. In conquering the vast wilderness and carving out new commonwealths America has had other wars to wage and battles to win beside those of a military nature. Of the 78 statues thus far presented by the states it is revealed that 45 of them represent men who had been Members of one or both branches of the Congress of the United States or of its predecessor, the Continental Congress. Of the 45 state-selected who had been Members of Congress, 9 had served in the Continental Congress, that is, prior to the formation of the Constitution of 1787 or the beginning of the new government in 1789. Thirty had high military service.

In the middle decades of the last century, including the Civil War period, several of the men from southern states served under more than one flag in more than one war, as for instance, some like Robert E. Lee served under the Stars and Stripes in the Mexican War and later under the Stars and Bars (the Confederate Flag) during the War Between the States. Some like General Joe Wheeler, served under the Stars and Stripes in the Spanish-American War after having earlier fought on the side of the Southern Confederacy. Since under the Law of 1864 concerning these statues each state exercises its own choice of two, it is significant to note that Virginia—out of her many illustrious sons—sent General Robert E. Lee to stand beside General George Washington in this great assemblage.

Perhaps it is because the statesman predominates over the soldier in our American life that these men in bronze and marble, even though in life they may have been distinguished military leaders, are chiefly dressed in civilian clothes. A foreign visitor passing along Unter Den Linden in Berlin and noting the many war-like figures might well say: "Prussia was hatched from a cannon ball like an eagle from an egg." But that same visitor passing through our National Statuary Hall at Washington and noting the preponderance of civilian dress and the garments of professional and work-a-day life could well say: "America apparently was born in toil and industry and became great through wise legislation and good counsel of her thinkers."

America does not yet show so many varieties of greatness as may be found at Westminster Abbey among England's Immortals, the explanation of which is rather obvious because of our young country. However the States have indicated great variety as they have varied their choices. Arizona has sent her coatless engineer and Pennsylvania her steam-boat inventor. Not to be outdone by these, Florida, Georgia and Kentucky furnished humanitarian geniuses who helped to alleviate human suffering and make life easier. In contrast to military glory Alabama and North Carolina offered educational leaders who have raised the general level of American culture. Further, in the realm of mind and spirit, Illinois sent her great woman reformer and Oklahoma presented two "Original Americans" whose unique abilities had improved the minds and bolstered the spirits of those with whom they lived and labored. This is as it should be to portray the varied character of American life and her amazing story of development.

Viewed by Hon. J. H. Birch; "It was a grand and patriotic conception which led to the dedication of this Hall. It had been hallowed by the presence of the great spirits who cemented the foundations of American Liberty and it is proper that the unborn generations who shall tread its sacred floor may read the history of the past in the silent statues gathered there."

Congressman James Buchanan of New Jersey expressed the hope that "as others come after us, to fill the places we occupy here and whose mission it shall be to take up the work of legislation where we lay it down —as they pass and repass among those reminders of other men and other days, of great deeds and noble action, of wise statesmanship and of heroic courage, may the God of Nations, the God of Battle, give them to see and to apprehend something of the spirit of wisdom and of statesmanship in which our fathers laid the foundations of the Republic, and something of the spirit of devotion to the Union which gave life and everything to its preservation, and so seeing and so apprehending may they discharge most wisely and in His fear the duties devolved upon them."

Such an invocation is a fitting thought, not only for Congressmen, but for all citizens, young and old, who seriously visit National Statuary Hall in the Capitol Building of the United States.

JOHN R. MURDOCK

Statues in the Capitol Building Given by the States

Page

14 ALABAMA
    General Joe Wheeler
    Jabez Lamar Monroe Curry

16 ARKANSAS
    Uriah M. Rose
    James P. Clarke

88 ARIZONA
    John Campbell Greenway

18 CALIFORNIA
    Junipero Serra
    Thomas Starr King

20 CONNECTICUT
    Roger Sherman
    Jonathan Trumbull

22 DELAWARE
    Caesar Rodney
    John M. Clayton

24 FLORIDA
    Dr. John Gorrie
    E. Kirby Smith

26 GEORGIA
    Alexander H. Stephens
    Dr. Crawford W. Long

28 IDAHO
    George L. Shoup
    William E. Borah

30 ILLINOIS
    Frances E. Willard
    James Shields

32 INDIANA
    General Lew Wallace
    Oliver P. Morton

Page

34 IOWA
    Samuel J. Kirkwood
    James Harlan

36 KANSAS
    John J. Ingalls
    George W. Glick

38 KENTUCKY
    Henry Clay
    Dr. Ephraim McDowell

88 LOUISIANA
    Huey Pierce Long

40 MAINE
    Hannibal Hamlin
    William King

42 MARYLAND
    Charles Carroll
    John Hanson

44 MASSACHUSETTS
    Samuel Adams
    John Winthrop

46 MICHIGAN
    Lewis Cass
    Zachariah Chandler

90 MINNESOTA
    Henry Mower Rice

48 MISSISSIPPI
    Jefferson Davis
    James Zachariah George

50 MISSOURI
    Thomas H. Benton
    Francis P. Blair

Page

52 NEBRASKA
    William Jennings Bryan
    J. Sterling Morton

54 NEW HAMPSHIRE
    Daniel Webster
    John Stark

56 NEW JERSEY
    Richard Stockton
    Philip Kearny

58 NEW YORK
    Robert R. Livingston
    George Clinton

60 NORTH CAROLINA
    Zebulon Baird Vance
    Charles Brantley Aycock

62 OHIO
    William Allen
    James A. Garfield

64 OKLAHOMA
    Sequoya
    Will Rogers

66 OREGON
    Reverend Jason Lee
    Dr. John McLoughlin

68 PENNSYLVANIA
    Robert Fulton
    John Peter Gabriel Muhlenberg

70 RHODE ISLAND
    Roger Williams
    Nathaniel Greene

Page

72 SOUTH CAROLINA
    John C. Calhoun
    Wade Hampton

90 SOUTH DAKOTA
    William Henry Harrison Beadle

74 TENNESSEE
    John Sevier
    Andrew Jackson

76 TEXAS
    Sam Houston
    Stephen F. Austin

92 UTAH
    Brigham Young

78 VERMONT
    Ethan Allen
    Jacob Collamer

80 VIRGINIA
    Robert E. Lee
    George Washington

92 WASHINGTON
    Marcus Whitman

82 WEST VIRGINIA
    Francis H. Pierpont
    John E. Kenna

84 WISCONSIN
    Robert Marion LaFollette
    James Marquette

States not Represented
COLORADO, MONTANA, NEVADA, NEW MEXICO, NORTH DAKOTA, WYOMING

Statues Not Given by States

96 Edward Dickinson Baker — Purchased 1873

96 Benjamin Franklin — Commission 1863

98 General Ulysses S. Grant — Gift 1900

98 Alexander Hamilton — Commission 1868

100 John Hancock — Commission 1861

100 Thomas Jefferson (m) — Commission 1855

102 Thomas Jefferson (b) — Gift 1834

102 Abraham Lincoln — Commission 1871

National Statuary Hall

THE CAR OF HISTORY

The Car of History with Clio, the Muse who presides over history, standing in a winged chariot and recording the passing events of the Nation is merely an accessory to the old House of Representatives' clock. The wheels indicate the flight of time as the car rolls over a globe encircled by the signs of the zodiac. This artistic bit of carved marble was done by Carlo Franzoni in 1819. When the House of Representatives moved to its present Chamber in 1857 the old "Franzoni clock" was left behind as an integral part of the old House of Representatives' Chamber, now NATIONAL STATUARY HALL.

GENERAL JOE WHEELER

1836-1906

Sculptor, BERTOLD NEBEL

JABEZ LAMAR MONROE CURRY

1825-1903

Sculptor, DANTE SODINI

Alabama

GENERAL JOE WHEELER

He had most unbelievable war records in three wars under two flags

SOLDIER, STATESMAN
Born in Augusta, Georgia, 1836
Attended Episcopal Academy, Connecticut
Graduated from West Point, 1859
Lieutenant, U. S. Army against Indians
Resigned commission, U. S. Army, 1861
Colonel, Alabama Infantry at Shiloh, 1862
Major general, Confederate Army, 1863
Cavalry general, Confederate Armies, 1864
After war, admitted to bar, Wheeler, Ala.
Member, U. S. H. of R., 1881-82; 1885-1900
Spanish-Am. War, 1898; Philippines, 1899
Retired; traveled in Europe, Mexico, 1900
Wrote books; died, Brooklyn, N. Y., 1906
Buried in Arlington National Cemetery
Bronze statue unveiled at Capitol, 1925
Statue located in Statuary Hall

General Wheeler was born in Georgia, but he lived in Alabama during the period of his life when the greater part of his service was rendered... He was a fighting general, always at the front where danger was greatest, leading his men and inspiring them by his own valor... Bright and glorious as is the record of General Wheeler in war, it can never be more beautiful or resplendent than his service to his State during the period of reconstruction. When the armies of the Confederacy went down in defeat, General Wheeler, with the same courage that had characterized his conduct on the field of battle accepted bravely and without murmur the result of the conflict and went back home to engage in the struggle to bring order out of chaos, to free his people from misrule and usurpation, and to set his State once more on the glad highway of peace and happiness.— Hon. Henry Bascom Steagall, M.C. of Alabama. *From unveiling ceremony*, March 12, 1925.

J. L. M. CURRY

He supported with positive action the cause of general education in the South

SOLDIER, STATESMAN, EDUCATOR
Born in Lincoln County, Georgia, 1825
Influence: Horace Mann; John C. Calhoun
Graduate, Georgia State University, 1843
Studied Law, Harvard; admitted to bar, 1845
With Texas Rangers, War with Mexico, 1846
Member, Ala. Legislature, 1847, 1853, 1855
Member, U. S. H. of R., 1857-61 (resigned)
Member, Confederate Congress, 1861-64
Lt. colonel, 5th Alabama Cavalry, 1864-65
President, Howard College (Alabama) 1865-68
English Prof., Richmond College, Va. 1868-81
Elected agent of Peabody Fund, 1881
Minister to Spain, 1885-88; Ambassador, 1902
Died in N. C., 1903; buried, Richmond, Va.
Marble statue accepted by Congress, 1908
Statue located in Hall of Columns

George Peabody, of old New England stock, made a gift of two million dollars to quicken schools of the South. Barnas Sears, the first agent of the Peabody fund, requested that Curry should be his successor because, "He is so many sided, so clear in his views, so judicious, and knows so well how to deal with all classes of men. His whole being is wrapped up in general education, and he is the best lecturer or speaker on the subject in all the South"... John F. Slater of Norwich Connecticut gave a million dollars in 1882 for negro schools in the South. Rutherford B. Hayes in 1890 secured Curry as agent of this fund. Thus to Curry's strong hand had come the main threads of educational progress in the South... The vast educational effort represented by the work of these Boards may be considered, so far as the South is concerned, the culmination of Curry's sixty years' devotion to the cause of universal education.— Dictionary of American Biography

URIAH M. ROSE

1834-1913

Sculptor, F. W. RUCKSTULL

JAMES P. CLARKE

1854-1916

Sculptor, POMPEO COPPINI

Arkansas

URIAH M. ROSE

He was an ideal representative of culture in a western frontier community

> JURIST, WRITER, WORLD TRAVELER
> Born at Bradfordsville, Kentucky, 1834
> Inherited small estate from father, 1849
> As deputy Co. Clerk studied law at night
> Graduate, law school, Lexington, Ky., 1853
> Practiced law, Batesville, Ark., 1853-60
> Chancellor, Pulaski County, Ark., 1860
> To Little Rock for law partnership, 1865
> Author, "Digest of Arkansas Reports", 1867
> To Europe and world travel, 1872
> Author, "Constitution of Arkansas", 1891
> Charter member, American Bar Ass'n., 1901
> Delegate, second Peace Conference, 1907
> Appointed by Theodore Roosevelt
> Died in 80th year, 1913
> Marble statue placed in Capitol, 1917
> Statue located in Statuary Hall

Uriah M. Rose steadfastly refused office, and declined to allow his name to be used for the U. S. Senate when election was almost a certainty. Conspicuous as a scholar both in literature and in languages, he was justly called by Judge Jeremiah Black, the most scholarly lawyer in America. In addition to his great law library he has accumulated over 6000 volumes of literary works in several languages. His writings, speeches and public orations are marked by dignity and finished elegance.—THE NATIONAL CYCLOPAEDIA OF AMERICAN BIOGRAPHY.

U. M. Rose was for the lifetime of a generation the most cultured man at the American bar. His knowledge of literature and art was not greater than his comprehension of the principles of justice and equity, which form the basis of our social, industrial, and political system.—SENATOR JOSEPH T. ROBINSON, Arkansas. *From memorial address*, February 18, 1917.

JAMES P. CLARKE

A worthy official of his great State both in Little Rock and in Washington

> GOVERNOR, STATESMAN
> Born in Yazoo City, Mississippi, 1854
> To Tutwilder's Academy, Greenbrier, Ala.
> Graduate, U. of Va., Charlottesville, 1878
> (Received his law degree at this time)
> Admitted to the bar in Arkansas
> Opened law office at Helena, Arkansas, 1879
> Member, Arkansas House of R., 1886-1888
> Member, Arkansas State Senate, 1888-1892
> Arkansas Attorney General, 1892-1894
> Governor of Arkansas, 1895-1896
> Moved to Little Rock and law practice
> In United States Senate, 1903-1916
> President pro tem in Senate, 1913, 1915
> Died, Little Rock, Ark., 1916; buried there
> Marble statue placed in Capitol, 1921
> Statue located in Hall of Columns

It is my good fortune to have known Senator Clarke all my life and to be familiar with the mainsprings of both his public and private conduct. They were integrity, courage, absolute independence, and consequent masterful will power. His public carreer was long. There was never an hour of it when his character and conduct were not under the scrutiny of friends and enemies, notwithstanding his detestation of notoriety; yet he was never suspected of dishonesty or of wilful disloyalty to the public interests. He was always observed and frequently assailed but never was his personal or official integrity impeached or questioned. He once said to me, "I have some confidences but no secrets." He did not fear to take any stand, to advance against any measure which his judgment condemned, or to spring to the support of any principle which his conscience approved. He was the only public man I ever knew whom I regarded as absolutely free from demagoguery. —SENATOR JOSEPH T. ROBINSON, Arkansas. *From memorial address*, February 18, 1917.

JUNIPERO SERRA

1713-1784

Sculptor, ETTORE CADORIN

THOMAS STARR KING

1824-1864

Sculptor, HAIG PATIGIAN

18

California

JUNIPERO SERRA

He led the Forces of Spanish Civilization and Christianity in subduing California

> SPANISH MISSIONARY, COLONIZER
> Born on island of Majorca, Spain, 1713
> Entered Franciscan Order, 1729
> Became eloquent pulpit orator
> Crossed Atlantic to Mexico, 1749
> Entered San Fernando College, Mexico City
> Missionary to Indians, Sierra Gorda, 1750
> His Order succeeded the Jesuits, 1767
> Went to Lower California, 1769
> Founded first Calif. Mission, San Diego
> Headquarters, San Carlos de Carmel
> Established 9 Missions in 15 years
> In governmental role as well as religious
> Died at Headquarters Mission, 1784
> Buried 'neath arches, San Carlos de Carmel
> Bronze statue unveiled at Capitol, 1931
> Statue Located in Statuary Hall

Junipero Serra was a man of greatness in simplicity, of outstanding accomplishment amid discouragement, of untiring zeal in the cause of religion, of unremitting effort on behalf of civilization... For nigh on sixteen years, this able, simple, kindly friar toiled in California. Up and down the coast on foot he traveled, an invalid physically. He taught the native Indians the homely arts of husbandry; he instilled into them the rudiments of government in frontier society; he brought to them the civilizing message of Christian belief and ethics. He prepared the slopes of this western land for the advantages of empire which years later was to press on and fructify. —Hon. Isidore B. Dockweiler, of Calif. *From unveiling ceremony*, March 1, 1931.

At the head of the missionary enterprise went Junipero Serra, a man remarkable among all pioneers in American history.... He showed himself a man of force who knew what he was talking about. — Herbert E. Bolton, Historian. *From Anza's California Expeditions.*

THOMAS STARR KING

He well and fittingly represented the early Anglo-American efforts in California

> PREACHER, PATRIOT, ORATOR
> Born in New York City, 1824
> With parents to Charlestown, Mass. 1835
> Worked as grocery clerk, 1836-1840
> Prepared for ministry, self directed
> Teacher, town school, Medford, Mass. 1840
> Principal, same school, Medford, Mass. 1842
> Ordained as Minister, 1846
> Pastor, Unitarian Church, Boston, 1848-1859
> Moved to San Francisco, Calif. 1860
> Traveled there via Isthmus of Panama
> Devoted follower of Abraham Lincoln
> Turned tide in Calif. for the Union
> (In Civil War both sides coveted Calif.)
> Died in San Francisco, 1864
> Bronze statue unveiled at Capitol, 1931
> Statue Located in Hall of Columns

Thomas Starr King at the beginning of the Civil War, found the people of his adopted state, (Calif.) then without transcontinental connection or communication, far removed from the center of discussion, uncertain as to her future course. With dauntless purpose and high enthusiasm, he entered the momentous struggle there, and by his matchless eloquence and indefatigable labors, he contributed in great measure to maintaining California as a member of the Federal Union and earned for himself the immortal epitaph, "He saved his State to the Union..." This scholarly, magestic, witty, radiant orator and devoted follower of Lincoln rode day and night from town to town, from mountain to sea, in this great domain, pleading to preserve the unity of the States, hammering at the shackles of slavery boldly, confidently, brilliantly, captivating the hearts and minds of men, kindling the spirit of "one Union indivisible" into a living patriot flame.—Ray Lyman Wilbur, Sec'y of the Interior. *From unveiling ceremony*, March 1, 1931.

ROGER SHERMAN

1721-1793

Sculptor, CHAUNCEY B. IVES

JONATHAN TRUMBULL

1710-1785

Sculptor, CHAUNCEY B. IVES

Connecticut

ROGER SHERMAN

The only "Founding Father" who signed all four of America's first State Papers

> SIGNER, DECL. OF INDEPENDENCE
> Born in Newton, Massachusetts, 1721
> From public schools to shoemaker's trade
> With family to New Milford, Conn., 1743
> Surveyor, 1745; Admitted to bar, 1754
> In Conn. Assembly, 1755-56, 1758-61, 1764-66
> Superior Court Judge, 1766-67, 1773-88
> In Continental Congress, 1774-81, 1783-84
> Signer, Declaration of 1774, non-trade pact
> Signer, Declaration of Independence, 1776
> Signer, Articles of Confederation, 1777
> Signer, United States Constitution, 1787
> Member, House of R., First Congress, 1789-91
> Member, U. S. Senate, 1791, till death
> Died, New Haven, Conn., 1793; buried there
> Marble statue accepted by Congress, 1872
> Statue located in Statuary Hall

. . . It is from the part which he took in the Convention of 1787 that Mr. Sherman is most known at the present day. His influence in that body was great, and increased as his associates became more familiar with his qualities. He seems to have regarded the work to be accomplished there in a two-fold aspect: first, to form a more perfect Union; and, second, so far as was compatible with such efficiency, to preserve the functions of the State governments. These ends he kept steadily in view though not refusing to yield his own opinions as to the method of attaining them. He spoke often, but always briefly and when excitement reached the height of angry feeling, and threatened to frustrate the objects of the Convention, he was able to reconcile the contending parties without sacrificing his own convictions. This power was mainly exerted in his intercourse with the members outside the Convention after its daily sessions were over.—SENATOR ORRIS SANFORD FERRY, Connecticut. *From The Congressional Globe*, March 8, 1872.

JONATHAN TRUMBULL

As patriotic Revolutionary War Governor he greatly inspired and aided Gen. Washington

> SOLDIER, STATESMAN, GOVERNOR
> Born in Lebanon, Connecticut, 1710
> Graduated from Harvard University, 1727
> He was licensed to preach the Gospel, 1731
> Business aptitude; entered politics early
> In Conn. Legislature, 1733-66 (intermittent)
> Served as Speaker of Assembly, three times
> Deputy Governor of Conn., 1766-1769
> Not a lawyer, yet held high judicial offices
> Spurned Writs of Assistance as Chief Justice
> Governor of Conn. 15 years, 1769-1784
> Washington's reliance during the Revolution
> He pled and worked for a "stronger Union"
> Had six children, including John the artist
> Died at Lebanon, Connecticut, 1785
> Marble statue accepted by Congress, 1872
> Statue located in House Connection

Jonathan Trumbull was the stern, uncompromising opponent of every measure that involved the liberties and rights of the American people. He was denounced by the King as the rebel Governor of Connecticut, a title that was intended as a reproach, but in reality was a high and honorable distinction. . . It was a distinguished honor that John Trumbull had the confidence and enjoyed the friendship of Washington. He was his most frequent and wisest counselor. . . In the hours of thick darkness when dangers were greatest, when the cause of the Colonies appeared the most hopeless, there was no want of faith in final success, no faltering in the heart of Trumbull, and no relaxation of efforts. For good sense and sound judgment, for the clearness of his convictions, for firmness of purpose, for executive ability, and for far-reaching statesmanship, he was the peer of Washington, and had no superior in that age. He was a Christian statesman. — SENATOR WILLIAM ALFRED BUCKINGHAM, Connecticut. *From The Congressional Globe*, Mar. 8, 1872.

CAESAR RODNEY

1728-1784

Sculptor, BRYANT BAKER

JOHN M. CLAYTON

1796-1856

Sculptor, BRYANT BAKER

Delaware

CAESAR RODNEY

He signed the Declaration of Independence, then strove to make it effective

> SIGNER, DECL. OF INDEPENDENCE
> Born in Kent County, Delaware, 1728
> Formal education limited; father died, 1745
> Dover citizen became Caesar's guardian
> Became High Sheriff of Kent County, 1755
> Del. lawmaker, 1762-69; Del. Justice, 1769-77
> Member of Continental Congress, 1774-1776
> One of 3 Delaware signers of Declaration
> Fought in Revolutionary Army as colonel
> Commissioned major general in 1777
> In command at the Battle of Trenton
> Member of Continental Congress, 1777-1778
> "President of Delaware," 1778-1782
> Never married; died near Dover, Del., 1784
> Buried, Christ Episcopal Churchyard, Dover
> Marble statue unveiled at Capitol, 1934
> Statue located in Statuary Hall

When the Delaware Statues' Commission finally came to grips with the question of selection, two rules were adopted. The first was that we should select persons that had had no connection with either of the major parties of the present day; and the second, that we should select men who were born in Delaware, lived in Delaware, and died and were buried in Delaware. So we honored one who helped to found a State and our Nation, and another whose great abilities were devoted to the healthy development and growth of Delaware, and of the United States. . . . Caesar Rodney was one of Delaware's greatest sons, the principal founder of our State as a political entity, independent of Pennsylvania, and one of a galaxy of distinguished men who in a time of great stress and danger were not afraid to think nobly and to act courageously when they severed the tie of the mother country with her colonies.—DR. GEORGE H. RYDEN, University of Delaware. *From the unveiling ceremony,* June 26, 1934.

JOHN M. CLAYTON

Co-author of the Clayton-Bulwer Treaty, historic in western hemispheric commerce

> JURIST, STATESMAN, DIPLOMAT
> Born in Dagsboro, Delaware, 1796
> Early schooling at Berlin, Maryland
> Entered Yale College at age of 15
> Graduate, Yale College, high honors, 1815
> Attended law school, Litchfield, Conn.
> Set up law office, Dover, Delaware, 1819
> Auditor of accounts for Delaware, 1821
> Member, Delaware House of R., 1824
> Secretary of State of Delaware, 1826-28
> Member, U. S. Senate, 1829-36; 1845-49
> Chief Justice of Delaware, 1837-1839
> Secretary of State (by Pres. Taylor), 1849
> Member, United States Senate, 1853-56
> Died at Dover, Delaware, 1856
> Marble statue unveiled at Capitol, 1934
> Statue located in Senate Connection

. . . The heroic dead of the Commonwealth of Delaware still live in the hearts of the States, which are forever united under the folds of one flag, one government, and one national ideal. — REV. JAMES SHERA MONTGOMERY, Chaplain of the House of Representatives. *From invocation at presentation of statues,* June 26, 1934.

Physically, John M. Clayton is described as a remarkably handsome man, 6 feet, 1½ inches tall, well proportioned, impressive in appearance, a splendid head, a benign countenance which bespoke the greatness of his soul, as his portraits reveal. . . . Few equaled him and none exceeded him in his knowledge of the law. He was a powerful advocate, a cross-examiner not to be denied, and an eloquent pleader before a jury. . . . He has always been considered one of the greatest chief justices of our State. No appeal was ever taken from his decisions. — HON. ROBERT G. HOUSTON, M. C. of Delaware. *From address at presentation of statues,* June 26, 1934.

JOHN GORRIE, M.D.

1802-1855

Sculptor, C. ADRIAN PILLARS

GENERAL E. KIRBY SMITH

1824-1893

Sculptor, C. ADRIAN PILLARS

Florida

DR. JOHN GORRIE

He made hot countries livable by his invention of mechanical ice making

PHYSICIAN, INVENTOR
Born on the island of St. Nevis, 1802
With parents moved to Charleston, S. C., 1803
Early education in Charleston, S. C.
Graduate, Medical School, N. Y. City, 1833
Settled in Apalachicola, Florida, 1833
Postmaster, Apalachicola, 1834; mayor, 1837
Resigned to give full time to medicine
Wrote, *Prevention of Malarial Diseases,* 1844
Tried for lower temperatures in sick rooms
This led to air conditioning and ice making
First mechanical refrigeration patent, 1851
Author, *Artificial Production of Ice,* 1854
Nervous collapse at financial failure
Died at home (at 53) in Apalachicola, 1855
Marble statue unveiled in Capitol, 1914
Statue located in Statuary Hall

Throughout the ages men have placed statues, erected monuments and established other memorials in an effort to preserve human achievement. Names, birth, and dates of death, with generous inscriptions, are not sufficient to distinguish the objects of the honor for their historic renown. Experience has taught this. Something of the man must be known.... Dr. Gorrie developed the first process for air conditioning. He completed the work of air conditioning the sick wards in the hospital, but he took no thought of fame or fortune. His paramount concern was for the sick. Cooling hospital wards was of more importance than the commercial possibilities of his ice-making machine.... His days were busy days. He found time, however, for social and civic contacts. He made friends. He served as treasurer of the city; a time as postmaster; secretary of the city's first Masonic Lodge; and was an incorporator and helped build Trinity Episcopal Church. — SENATOR CLAUDE PEPPER, Florida. *From Congressional Record,* April 24, 1940.

GENERAL E. KIRBY SMITH

He held out longest for the "Lost Cause" then returned to his first loyalty

SOLDIER, EDUCATOR
Born at St. Augustine, Florida, 1824
Father, Judge of District Court, 1823-37
Father, commissioned officer in War of 1812
Graduated, West Point with honors, 1845
Assigned to 5th Infantry, War with Mexico
Teacher, mathematics at West Point, 1849-52
Army escort, Mexican Boundary Com., 1852
Florida seceded; Kirby Smith resigned, 1861
Lt. colonel of Cavalry (by Jefferson Davis)
Lt. general, 1862; full general, 1864
His the last Confederate force to surrender
Chancellor, U. of Nashville, Tenn., 1870-75
Teacher of math. at U. of Sewanee, 1875-93
Died at Sewanee, Tennessee, 1893
Bronze statue placed in Capitol, 1918
Statue located in Hall of Columns

Mr. Speaker, I ask unanimous consent to address the House for 5 minutes on a concurrent resolution accepting the statue of Gen. E. Kirby Smith.... As my colleagues know, I have never made a sectional speech since I have been in Congress.... As I have often stated, there should be no North, no East, no South, no West, and we should be a united Union, as our people are one, and the making of sectional speeches can but do harm.... I quote a resolution which was passed by the Confederate Congress, 1864: "Resolved, That Gen. E. Kirby Smith has distinguished his administration of the trans-Mississippi department by his justice, his firmness and moderation, his integrity and conscientious regard for law, his unaffected kindness to the people, the protection of their rights and the redress of their wrongs, and has thus won the confidence of Congress. That the thanks of Congress are due and are extended to Gen. E. Kirby Smith." — HON. WILLIAM JOSEPH SEARS, M.C. of Florida. *From The Congressional Record,* January 25, 1922.

ALEXANDER H. STEPHENS	CRAWFORD W. LONG, M.D.
1812-1883	1815-1878
Sculptor, GUTZON BORGLUM	*Sculptor,* J. MASSEY RHIND

Georgia

ALEXANDER H. STEPHENS

He loved the American Union but he loved more his sovereign state of Georgia

> PARLIAMENTARIAN, STATESMAN
> Born near Crawfordville, Georgia, 1812
> Graduate, the University of Georgia, 1832
> Taught school 18 months; studied law
> Admitted to bar in Crawfordville, 1834
> Member, Georgia House of R., 1836-1841
> Served in Georgia State Senate, 1842
> Member, U. S. House of R., 1843-1859
> Member, Georgia Secession Convention, 1861
> Elected Vice President of the Confederacy
> After the War, imprisoned for 5 months
> Member, U. S. H. of R., 1873-82 (resigned)
> Governor of Georgia, 1882, till death
> Died, 1883, in Atlanta, Georgia
> Buried on estate, Crawfordville, Georgia
> Marble statue unveiled in Capitol, 1927
> Statue located in Statuary Hall

No man in the world's history ever surpassed Alexander H. Stephens in the steadfastness of his devotion to the principles of truth, justice, and mercy. His private life was without fear and without reproach and full of incidents of helpfulness to those in need, especially to young men seeking aid to attend college. His public career shows him time and again placing his loyalty to principles above subservience to political party; time and again refusing to follow where he thought principles were being set aside for party purposes. On the tablet of his heart was written the sentence often quoted by him, "Times change and men change with them, but principles never." ... He was a great parliamentarian and a great orator. These gifts he devoted to the highest interest of his country, to the preservation of the Union and to the cause of Constitutional liberty. — SENATOR WILLIAM JULIUS HARRIS, Georgia. *From unveiling ceremony*, December 8, 1927.

DR. CRAWFORD W. LONG

He saved humanity untold suffering by introducing anesthesia in surgery

> PHYSICIAN, SURGEON
> Born in Danielsville, Georgia, 1815
> Both grandfathers fought in Revolution
> Admitted to Franklin College, at age of 14
> Franklin College now University of Georgia
> Graduate, Franklin College, M.A., 1835
> Alexander H. Stephens roommate at College
> Studied medicine at University of Penna.
> Received degree, Doctor of Medicine, 1839
> Worked in New York hospital till 1841
> Always perfecting his skill in surgery
> Located temporarily at Jefferson, Georgia
> First to use ether in surgery, 1842
> Became noted surgeon in Athens, Georgia
> Died at bedside of a patient, 1878
> Marble statue unveiled in Capitol, 1926
> Statue located in Senate Connection

As a pharmacist it was my great good fortune in my early days to be an apprentice and student in the drug store in the town of Athens, Georgia, owned and operated by the man whom we commemorate today, and I was the recipient of many kindnesses at his hands, and I am here to testify to the greatness of this man in every respect; as a physician, kind and gentle; as a friend, loyal and true; as a citizen, brave, wise, and patriotic. The skilled and gentle ministrations of the learned physician were his; the tender love for family and for friends he ever exhibited in acts of kindness; the poor and distressed found in him ever a ready and helpful sympathy; his city and state knew him as patriotic, brave, and wise. All the Nations of the earth commemorate this man, whose discovery lessened pain and the danger and terror of the surgeon's knife.—DR. JOSEPH JACOBS, former employee of Dr. Long. *From unveiling ceremony,* March 30, 1926.

GEORGE L. SHOUP

1836-1904

Sculptor, F. E. TRIEBELL

WILLIAM E. BORAH

1865-1940

Sculptor, BRYANT BAKER

Idaho

GEORGE L. SHOUP

His ability as soldier, statesman, businessman, all served the great West

PIONEER, SOLDIER, STATESMAN
Born in Armstrong Co., Pennsylvania, 1836
Became farmer and stockman in Ill., 1852
Moved to Pike's Peak, Colorado, 1859
Became miner, merchant, prospector, 1859
Lieutenant, 1st Colorado Cavalry, 1863
Delegate, Colo. Ter. Const. Convention, 1864
Colonel, 3rd regiment Colo. Cavalry, 1864
To Salmon City, Idaho, after army discharge
Became successful miner, stockman, merchant
Member, Idaho Ter. legislature, 1874-1878
Governor, Territory of Idaho, 1889; 1890
Governor, State of Idaho, 1890 (resigned)
Member, United States Senate, 1890-1901
Died at Boise, Idaho, 1904; buried in Boise
Marble statue accepted by Congress, 1910
Statue located in Statuary Hall

I count it one of the good fortunes of my life to have known George L. Shoup—a man of action, of affairs, of tremendous force of will, and yet the characteristic that most impressed me in him was his unfailing good nature. No man had a keener sense of humor than he; few that I have met were more uniformly kind, cheerful, and optimistic; and yet no one could know him long without realizing the depth and firmness of the character that lay behind that kindly and smiling exterior. . . . We are proud to claim George L. Shoup as a characteristic American—hardy pioneer, valiant soldier, master builder in industry and statecraft, and, above and better than all else, one who was warm hearted, sympathetic, generous, and faithful in every relation of life. The State of Idaho has done well in placing the statue of George L. Shoup in the American Hall of Fame.—Hon. Franklin Wheeler Mondell, M.C. of Wyoming. *From The Congressional Record,* January 15, 1910.

WILLIAM E. BORAH

He was a frontier product, moving west with America's star of empire

STATESMAN, ORATOR
Born near Fairfield, Illinois, 1865
Attended common schools, Wayne Co., Ill.
Student, Southern Illinois Academy
Graduate, University of Kansas, 1889
Admitted to bar in Kansas, 1890
Began law practice in Lyons, Kansas
Moved law practice to Boise, Idaho, 1891
Lost candidacy to U. S. House of R., 1896
Member, U. S. Senate from Idaho, 1907-1940
Member, Republican Nat'l Com., 1908-1912
Delegate, Republican Nat'l Conv., 1912
Lost Presidential Nomination, 1936
Died, Washington, D. C., 1940
Buried, Morris Hill Cemetery, Boise, Ida.
Bronze statue unveiled at Capitol, 1947
Statue located in Senate Connection

William E. Borah grew in stature each succeeding year. He grew in influence which leaped the boundaries of his native land and spanned the earth. He grew in the talents which made him the greatest advocate and orator of his time. He became the Senate's dean—not alone in years of service, but equally in the personal prestige of a unique and mighty character which was worthy of the Senate in its richest tradition since the Government was born. He loved America and America loved him. He believed in America with a passion which was the touchstone of his life.—Senator Arthur H. Vandenberg, Michigan (1940).

We dare to pray that Thou wilt raise up among us men like him—men of independent mind, not bending to every varying wind, but standing stalwart as oaks for what they know to be right. Wilt thou bless this Nation, which he loved so much and served so well. — Rev. Peter Marshall, Chaplain, U. S. Senate (1947).

FRANCES E. WILLARD

1839-1898

Sculptor, HELEN FARNSWORTH MEARS

GENERAL JAMES SHIELDS

1810-1879

Sculptor, LEONARD W. VOLK

Illinois

FRANCES E. WILLARD

She dedicated her life and great ability to the cause of temperance

PHILANTHROPIST, REFORMER
Born in Churchville, N. Y., 1839
Ancestors noted before Revolutionary War
Willard family settled in Wisconsin, 1846
Graduate, Northwestern Female College
This College located in Evanston, Ilinois
It became part of Northwestern University
Pres. Evanston College for Ladies, 1871
First female College controlled by women
Resigned from Northwestern Univ., 1874
President, Illinois W.C.T.U., 1874
President, National W.C.T.U., 1879
President, World W.C.T.U., 1883
Distinguished civic service till death
Died in New York City, 1898
Marble statue accepted by Congress, 1905
Statue located in Statuary Hall

No man or woman of her time wrought better or accomplished more for the protection and upbuilding of her sex and the cause of temperance than Frances E. Willard. The endearments of home and the quiet of her fireside were sacrificed in the interest of the unfortunate among both men and women. . . . The cause for which she dedicated her life reaches all humanity. The ability with which she prosecuted this lifework places her among the most eminent intellects of our generation. She possessed all the qualities of organization which have made such men as Marshall Field, Morgan, and Carnegie multimillionaires; a genius which in military affairs would have made a general of the first rank; legislative qualities which in the statesman would have made his name historical; oratorical abilities which have made such men as Beecher and Spurgeon immortal; and a charity which was heaven-born.—SENATOR ALBERT J. HOPKINS, Illinois. *From The Congressional Record,* January 15, 1905.

GENERAL JAMES SHIELDS

He has the unique distinction of having represented three states in the U. S. Senate

SOLDIER, STATESMAN
Born, Ireland, 1810; classical education
Immigrated to Kaskaskia, Illinois, 1823
Admitted to bar, 1832; in Black Hawk War
Ill. legislator, 1836; Ill. auditor, 1839
Illinois Supreme Court Judge, 1843
Brig. general, Illinois volunteers, 1846
Member, U. S. Senate (from Ill.), 1849-55
Moved to land grant in Minnesota
Member, U. S. Senate (from Minn.), 1858-59
Moved to Calif.; brig. general, 1861-63
Resigned from Army, 1863; retired to Calif.
To Carrollton, Mo.; in Mo. H. of R., 1874-79
Member, U. S. Senate (from Mo.), 1879
Died on tour, 1879; buried, Carrollton, Mo.
Bronze statue accepted by Congress, 1893
Statue located in Hall of Columns

The simple recital of the wonderful career of General Shields seems almost like a dream of fancy. No other American citizen has ever been certified as a member of this Senate by three different great states. . . . While he was foreign born, yet no American citizen has ever shown greater affection for the Union and the flag; neither did any patriot show more willingness to spill his blood for human liberty. He was the close friend of Douglas, serving with him upon the Supreme bench of Illinois, and was also his colleague in this Senate. . . . He was the friend of the Union soldier, and his last period of service in the Senate was marked by his fervent appeal in behalf of the veterans of the Mexican War. . . . He was hero, patriot, soldier and statesman. He believed in his adopted country, and was ever ready to fight for its flag in war, as he always served it faithfully in peace.—SENATOR SHELBY MOORE CULLOM, Illinois. *From The Congressional Record,* December 6, 1893.

GENERAL LEW WALLACE

1827-1905

Sculptor, ANDREW O'CONNOR

OLIVER P. MORTON

1823-1877

Sculptor, C. H. NIEHAUS

Indiana

GENERAL LEW WALLACE

He was familiar with battlefields, high political offices and scholarly pursuits

SOLDIER, STATESMAN, AUTHOR
Born in Brookville, Indiana, 1827
Had every educational opportunity
Voluminous reader, great comand of language
Took part in Mexican War, 1847-1848
Member, Indiana State Senate, 1856-1860
Organized, drilled, military company, 1856
Adj. general, 1861; maj. general, 1862
"March, bivouac, battlefield," 1861-1865
To Crawfordsville, Ind. law office, 1865
Terr. Gov., N. M. (by Pres. Grant), 1878-81
Minister to Turkey (Pres. Garfield), 1881-85
Back to Crawfordsville law office, 1885
Author: *The Fair God,* 1873; *Ben Hur,* 1878
Died at Crawfordsville, Indiana, 1905
Marble statue unveiled in Capitol, 1910
Statue located in Statuary Hall

General Lew Wallace loved liberty for all men and he fought for it. He worshiped the Nation because of what the American Nation means; and to save the Nation he gladly offered his life on many a battlefield. He suggested laws for the betterment of human conditions. He wrote noble books, one of which, translated into every modern and even into one oriental tongue, has lifted all the civilized world nearer to the Saviour of mankind. . . . Lew Wallace was one of these fighting idealists; one of the men whose brain and heart took in the Nation, and therefore took in the hopes and aspirations of the common people of all the world. . . . So Indiana proudly unveils this statue of Lew Wallace—soldier and lawgiver, author and idealist, dreamer of beautiful dreams for better things for his fellow men; and wielder of sword and pen which helped those dreams come true. . . . His life bore fruit.—SENATOR ALBERT J. BEVERIDGE, Indiana. *From unveiling ceremony,* January 11, 1910.

OLIVER P. MORTON

As war governor he powerfully supported the embattled war president—Abraham Lincoln

WAR GOVERNOR, STATESMAN
Born in Saulsbury, Indiana, 1823
Early education frequently interrupted
Graduate, Miami U., Oxford, Ohio, 1845
Left College, began study of law, 1845
Admitted to the Indiana bar, 1847
Judge, sixth judicial circuit, Ind., 1852
Lieutenant Governor of Indiana, 1860
Served Indiana as Governor, 1861-1867
As war Governor equipped 200,000 soldiers
For Union Cause and President Lincoln
Member, U. S. Senate, 1867-1877
Member, Electoral Commission, 1876-1877
Heroic service marked his 10 Senate years
Died at Indianapolis, Indiana, 1877
Marble statue accepted by Congress, 1900
Statue located in Hall of Columns

Morton's whole career was based upon profound belief in the common people—the living, vital, human faith of one who in himself is of the people. That is why he was a Nationalist. That is why he sent that telegram to Lincoln the very hour the President called for troops—he believed the 10,000 men he tendered would respond. Faith is the heart of deeds. That was why he built arsenals, bought provisions, equipped a quarter of a million men for war—he believed the people would sustain him. That was why he pressed the ratification of the fourteenth amendment, and as a Senator, the adoption and ratification of the fifteenth amendment to the Constitution of the United States. That is why he championed reconstruction, based, as he declared, "upon the everlasting principles of equal and exact justice to all men."—SENATOR ALBERT J. BEVERIDGE, Indiana. *From The Congressional Record, the acceptance proceedings in the Senate,* April 14, 1900.

SAMUEL J. KIRKWOOD

1813-1894

Sculptor, VINNIE REAM HOXIE

JAMES HARLAN

1820-1899

Sculptor, NELLIE V. WALKER

Iowa

SAMUEL J. KIRKWOOD

Marylander by birth, pledged his fortune in Iowa for the Union cause

STATESMAN, WAR GOVERNOR
Born, Harford Co., Md., 1813; in wealth
Private school, Washington, 1823-1827
Teacher, drug clerk; family moved west
Settled in Richland County, Ohio
Taught school; admitted to the bar, 1843
Prosecuting att'y, Richland Co., 1845-49
Member, Ohio Constitutional Conv., 1850-51
Moved to Iowa, 1855; became farmer, miller
Iowa Governor, 1859; reelected, 1861
Pledged personal fortune in Union Cause
In U. S. Senate, 1866-67 (James Harlan term)
Governor, 1876; In U. S. Senate, 1877-81
Sec'y of Interior, by Pres. Garfield, 1881-82
Died at home in Iowa City, 1894
Marble statue erected in Capitol, 1913
Statue located in Statuary Hall

JAMES HARLAN

He was a University Professor turned United States Senator for sixteen years

STATESMAN, ORATOR, EDUCATOR
Born, Clark Co., Illinois, 1820
Family moved to Parke Co., Indiana, 1824
Graduated, Asbury U., Indiana, 1845
Teacher, Mo.; Prin., Iowa City College, 1846
Supt., Public Instruction, Iowa, 1847-1849
To bar, 1848; declined Gov. race, 1850
President, Iowa Wesleyan U., 1853-1855
Member, U. S. Senate, 1855-65 (resigned)
Sec'y of Interior, 1865 (resigned, 1866)
(Daughter married Robert Todd Lincoln)
Member, U. S. Senate, 1866-1872
President, Iowa Wesleyan U., 1869-1870
Presiding Judge on Alabama Claims, 1882-86
Died in Mount Pleasant, Iowa, 1899
Bronze statue erected in Capitol, 1910
Statue located in Hall of Columns

Mr. President, I rise to say a few words only. First of all I want to express to the Senator from Iowa, Mr. Kirkwood, the great gratification I have felt in listening to his speech. He has made an able, a dignified, and an excellent speech, worthy of a Senator anywhere and in any age. If all the speeches made on this floor were made in the same spirit and with the same clearness and patriotic temper which the Senator has exhibited, I think what he intimated as doubtful would never be doubtful again, and that is, whether this is a dignified body.... I want my friend to know and I want his people to know that the patriotic, the manly, the catholic, the national, the unsectional sentiments which fell from his lips, and which I know animate his bosom, meet with a warm and hearty response in mine and in the bosoms of my people.—SENATOR BENJAMIN J. HILL, Georgia. *From The Congressional Record,* June 20, 1879.

Mr. Harlan was highly esteemed throughout his senatorial career for his practical wisdom as a statesman, his influence and power in debate and his captivating oratory. It is said of him that whenever he spoke on the existing issues of the time he always called out the ablest democratic members in reply — such Senators as Stephen Douglas and Louis Cass. The Governor of Illinois said of him, "Mr. Harlan makes the best campaign speeches of anyone in the State." He was called the most successful passer of bills, and Charles Sumner esteemed him so highly that he requested the Senate, who placed him on the Committee of Foreign Relations, to make Mr. Harlan Chairman. Roscoe Conklin said of Mr. Harlan, "He is the strongest, most convincing debater I have ever listened to, one of the really great men who have served in the Senate ..." Altogether, Mr. Harlan was considered the most powerful political speaker Iowa introduced to the Country. — *National Cyclopaedia of American Biography.*

JOHN J. INGALLS

1833-1900

Sculptor, C. H. NIEHAUS

GEORGE W. GLICK

1827-1911

Sculptor, C. H. NIEHAUS

Kansas

JOHN JAMES INGALLS

He was a worthy New England contribution to the worth of Kansas

> ORATOR, STATESMAN
> Born in Middleton, Massachusetts, 1833
> Graduate, Williams College, Mass., 1855
> Admitted to the bar in Massachusetts, 1857
> Moved to the Territory of Kansas, 1858
> Member, Kansas Constitutional Conv., 1859
> Secretary, Kansas Territorial Council, 1860
> Secretary, Kansas State Senate, 1861
> Commissioned Judge Advocate, 1863-1865
> Ranks: major and lieutenant colonel
> Member, United States Senate, 1873-1891
> Last years: journalism, literature, farming
> Last words: "Thy kingdom come."
> Died, East Las Vegas, New Mexico, 1900
> Buried, Mount Vernon Cemetery, Atchison
> Marble statue accepted by Congress, 1905
> Statue located in Statuary Hall

John James Ingalls was a colossal figure on the stage of our affairs. There may have been orators as eloquent, statesmen as wise, politicians as courageous, citizens as patriotic and devoted, but I recall few, if any, who, as orator, statesman, politician, and patriot, united in one person so many of these virtues in such conspicuous manifestations. He was a master of our language. He made of it a splendid yet a docile instrument. Logic, pathos, fascination, invective, and entreaty—these forces he employed at will and irresistibly. His speech was clear, incisive, musical, and luminous. His arguments were always persuasive and enlightened, his motives transparently high and pure. His denunciations were terrible, his irony a blight. He hated deceit, hypocrisy, pretense and cowardice. He laid a ruthless hand on treachery and meanness; he treated with his scorn the fawning knee. He loved his country with unbounded passion. He worshiped justice, candor, patriotism.—Senator Arthur P. Gorman, Maryland. *From The Congressional Record,* January 21, 1905.

GEORGE W. GLICK

He contributed greatly to the westward movement of our Star of Empire

> PIONEER, STATESMAN
> Born in Greencastle, Ohio, 1827
> Both grandfathers served in War of 1812
> Early schooling near Fremont, Ohio
> Law student with Buckland & Hayes at 21
>   (Rutherford B. Hayes member of this firm)
> Admitted to bar in Cincinnati, 1850
> Located in Atchison, Kansas, 1859
> Helped prepare Kansas Constitution
> Democrat in Kansas Legislature, 1862-80
> Speaker, Kansas House of R., 1876
> Democratic Governor of Kansas, 1882-84
> Appointed pension agent at Topeka, 1885
> Followed farming and stockraising 30 years
> Died at his home in Atchison, 1911
> Marble statue accepted by Congress, 1914
> Statue located in Hall of Columns

Governor Glick had the respect and esteem of Kansas people of all parties. His sagacity and courage in treating public questions, his detestation of trickery, and his fair treatment of all won and kept him loyal friends. His inflexible determination to make Kansas respected and entitled to the respect of the Nation forced him into a position of prominence and responsibility. His unswerving attitude through all the changes and vicissitudes of the State made his name a household word. More than to any other man is due the credit for construction of the important railroads of the State of Kansas. He was charter member of the Atchison, Topeka and Santa Fe organization, which line started from the city of Atchison as its eastern terminus. He helped to build up the farming industries of the State, and was always consulted in all matters of farming and stockraising. His natural instincts were in harmony with an agricultural region . . . —Senator William Howard Thompson, Kansas. *From The Congressional Record,* June 24, 1914.

37

HENRY CLAY

1777-1852

Sculptor, C. H. NIEHAUS

EPHRAIM McDOWELL, M.D.

1771-1830

Sculptor, C. H. NIEHAUS

Kentucky

HENRY CLAY

He belonged to Kentucky, the great West, America, and to the World

    STATESMAN, PARLIAMENTARIAN
    Born, Hanover Co., Va. (The Slashes), 1777
    Studied law, Va.; to bar, 1797; Ky. practice
    Member, Kentucky House of R., 1803
    Filled U. S. Senate vacancy, 1806-1807
    Member, Kentucky House of R., 1808-1809
    Filled U. S. Senate vacancy, 1810-1811
    Member, U. S. H. of R. (Speaker), 1811-14
    Peace Commissioner to Great Britain, 1814
    Member, U. S. H. of R. (Speaker), 1815-21
    Member, U. S. H. of R., 1823-25 (resigned)
    Secretary of State (by Pres. Adams), 1825-29
    Member, U. S. Senate, 1831-37; 1837-42
    Candidate for Presidencey, 1824; 1832; 1844
    Member, U. S. Senate, 1849-1852; died, 1852
    Bronze statue unveiled in Capitol, 1929
    Statue located in Statuary Hall

Today Henry Clay takes his place beside Webster, Calhoun, Benton, Cass and the immortal Jackson whose figures in chiseled marble and molded bronze stand in this hall dedicated by Act of Congress to the individual States as a shrine for the statues of the best loved among their illustrious dead. Here in Statuary Hall we ought to consecrate our lives to the service of our Country.... As an intrepid and inspiring party chieftain, as a resourceful and redoubtable parliamentary leader, as a magnetic and charming personality, as a brilliant and versatile orator, Henry Clay has had no equal in the annals of America.... In Henry Clay, nature mixed in perfect proportion all the elements that constitute a truly great orator. With his scintillating intellect, pure patriotism, physical, mental and moral courage, masterful personality, imperious nature, superb histrionic ability, naturalness of gesture, marvelous voice, and mastery of crowd psychology....—HON. VIRGIL CHAPMAN, M.C. of Kentucky. *From unveiling ceremony,* March 3, 1929.

DR. EPHRAIM McDOWELL

First surgeon ever to cut into abdominal cavity and remove ovarian tumor

    PIONEER, SCIENTIST, SURGEON
    Born, Rockbridge County, Virginia, 1771
    With parents to Danville, Kentucky, 1783
    Pupil, classical school, Georgetown, Va.
    Student of medicine, Staunton, Virginia
    Studied medicine, Edinburgh, Scotland, 1793
    Physician, surgeon, Danville, Kentucky, 1795
    Performed first abdominal operation, 1809
    Jane Crawford patient for this ovariotomy
    She rode 60 miles horseback for operation
    (Ether not used in surgery until 1842)
    Member, Philadelphia Medical Society, 1817
    Founder, Centre College, Danville, Ky., 1819
    Died in Danville, Kentucky, 1830
    Monument, McDowell Park, Danville, 1879
    Bronze statue unveiled in Capitol, 1929
    Statue located in Senate Connection

Dr. McDowell rode to the Hermitage, the home of Andrew Jackson, near Nashville, to perform an operation on a Mrs. Overton. The only assistance he had in the performance of this operation were Old Hickory himself and a woman who lived in the neighborhood. Dr. McDowell also performed a surgical operation on James K. Polk, who then lived in Tennessee.... He was a friend of the poor, the companion of the lowly and the great, and it offers a peculiar testimonial to the opportunities of American life to find his statue in this Hall of Fame with that of Andrew Jackson and other pioneer heroes who contributed to the wealth of history in the Republic of the United States.... The country doctor was more than a physician; he was counselor and friend. He enjoyed a confidence with the family, enjoyed by no other, and his part in the pioneer life of a growing and restless people deserves eternal commemoration in any Hall of Fame.—SENATOR ALBEN W. BARKLEY, Kentucky. *From unveiling ceremony,* March 3, 1929.

HANNIBAL HAMLIN

1809-1891

Sculptor, CHARLES E. TEFFT

WILLIAM KING

1768-1852

Sculptor, FRANKLIN SIMMONS

Maine

HANNIBAL HAMLIN

Alternately, political leader of both parties in Maine during tumultuous Civil War period

VICE PRESIDENT OF THE U. S.
Born, Paris, Oxford County, Maine, 1809
Schools: district and Hebron Academy
Managed the home farm until 21 years old
Member, Maine House of R., 1836-1840
Speaker, Me. House of R., 1837; 1839; 1840
Member, U. S. H. of R. (Democrat), 1843-47
Member, U. S. Senate (Democrat), 1848-1857
Republican Gov. of Maine, 1857 (resigned)
Member, U. S. Senate (Republican), 1857-61
Vice President of the U. S., 1861-1865
Collector, Port of Boston, 1865-1866
Member, U. S. Senate (Republican), 1869-81
U. S. Minister to Spain, 1881-82 (resigned)
Agriculturalist; died, Bangor, Me., 1891
Bronze statue unveiled in Capitol, 1935
Statue located in Statuary Hall

Coming to Congress in the years preceding that great strife between the States when America was entering that period of foment from which the Union finally emerged triumphant, Hannibal Hamlin was tested as were few men before our people. He, without curb on his thoughts, guided by his principles, and by ties of no kind, coming here under the name of the party which was then dominant, he found himself led inevitably by the events of those days, ultimately to transfer his allegiance to that new party dedicated to the principle of the Union as we now know it.... We shall do well if we are worthy of his service, to be ready ourselves to sacrifice those things that we may seem temporarily to hold most dear, in order that this Nation in this day shall have that new birth of freedom for which they were ready then to sacrifice their lives. — HON. RALPH O. BREWSTER, M.C. of Maine. *From The Congressional Record,* June 11, 1935.

WILLIAM KING

He laid the economic foundations of Maine, then obtained Statehood for her

INDUSTRIALIST, STATESMAN
Born, Scarboro, Maine, midst poverty, 1768
Little schooling but much hard work
Member, General Court in Boston, 1795-96
Member, Mass. Legislature, 1800-1803
State Senator, Lincoln District, 1807-08
Author: *Betterment Act; Toleration Act*
Leader in separating Maine from Mass.
Pres., Maine Constitutional Conv., 1819
Elected first Governor of Maine, 1820
Became Florida Claims Commissioner, 1821
Customs collector at Bath, 1831-1834
Became wealthy merchant and ship owner
Started first cotton textile mill in Maine
Died at Bath, Maine, 1852
Marble statue accepted by Congress, 1878
Statue located in House Connection

William King was the first governor of the State, and the universal contemporary judgment marked him foremost of the men of Maine of his time and generation, in all the intellectual and moral endowments which constitute individual greatness. In his public career he was the leader in memorable measures in vindication of religious freedom and the rights of labor, the influence of which was felt over the whole country.—SENATOR HANNIBAL HAMLIN, Maine. *From The Congressional Record,* January 22, 1878.

At the head of the movement to separate Maine from Massachusetts, its leader, its organizer, its patriotic and eloquent advocate was William King. He restrained the wrath of the imprudent, quickened the zeal of the laggard, dissipated the fears of the doubting, and molded his adherents and followers into a compact, cooperative, effective force.... He, more than any other man, created the State of Maine.—SENATOR JAMES G. BLAINE, Maine. *From Cong'l. Record,* Jan. 22, 1878.

CHARLES CARROLL

1737-1832

Sculptor, RICHARD E. BROOKS

JOHN HANSON

1715-1783

Sculptor, RICHARD E. BROOKS

Maryland

CHARLES CARROLL

He dared to give King George III the home address of one rebel

SIGNER, DECL. OF INDEPENDENCE
Born at Annapolis, Maryland, 1737
Father wealthy; Charles educated in Europe
Returned to Annapolis at age 28
Joined "Sons of Liberty," 1765
Commissioner to Canada, by Congress, 1776
Delegate to Continental Congress, 1776
Resigned from Congress at close of 1778
Member, Maryland Senate, 1777-1800
Member, U. S. Senate, 1st Congress, 1789-92
Public career as Federalist ended, 1801
Set stone for first B & O Railroad, 1828
Last years devoted to home and religion
Last surviving signer of The Declaration
Died in Baltimore, Maryland, 1832
Bronze statue accepted by Congress, 1903
Statue located in Statuary Hall

"Of the illustrious signers of the Declaration of Independence there now remains only one, Charles Carroll. He seems an aged oak, standing alone, on the plain, which time has spared a little longer after all of its contemporaries have been leveled with the dust. Venerable object! We delight to gather around its trunk while yet it stands, and to dwell beneath its shadow. Sole survivor of an assembly of as great men as the world has witnessed in a transaction, one of the most important that history records. What thoughts, what interesting reflections must fill his elevated and devout soul! If he dwell on the past, how touching its recollections; if he survey the present, how happy, how full of the fruition of that hope which his ardent patriotism indulged; if he glance at the future, how does the prospect of his Country's advancement almost bewilder his weakened conception! ... Fortunate, distinguished patriot!"—DANIEL WEBSTER, July 4, 1826. *From* SENATOR LOUIS E. MCCOMAS, *Delaware, in the U. S. Senate*, December 20, 1902.

JOHN HANSON

President of the Continental Congress, 1781; often called America's first President.

PATRIOT, STATESMAN
Born in Charles County, Maryland, 1715
Received academic education in Maryland
In Charles Co. Provincial Assembly 9 times
Member, Maryland State Senate, 1757-1773
Immigrated to Frederick County, 1773
Delegate, general Congress, Annapolis, 1774
Member, Continental Congress, 1780-83
President, Continental Congress, 1781-1782
Signer, Articles of Confederation, 1781
Officially thanked Washington for Yorktown
Leader, Md.'s transition, province to state
Retired from public service, 1782
Spent last days at Oxon Hill, Maryland
Died at home of nephew, Oxon Hill, 1783
Bronze statue accepted by Congress, 1903
Statue located in Senate Connection

The great labor accomplished (1782), independence won, and the nation in its formative period, with every indication of advancement and success, John Hanson, now a man old in years, as well as high in honors, retired from public life, seeking seclusion and rest. ... He was the first "President of the United States in Congress assembled," and his hand guided the fortunes of the new nation in the year which brought the final success of American arms, after a long period of changeful fortune. He was not a man of selfish ambition but became active in the affairs of his native colony by reason of his love of country and steadfast purpose to stand by and for the right. ... Only a high sense of duty kept him for five and twenty years constantly engaged in public service and allowed him to retire only when his fondest hopes had been realized in the consummation of freedom and self-government for his native land.—SENATOR GEORGE LOUIS WELLINGTON, Maryland. *From The Congressional Record*, January 31, 1903.

SAMUEL ADAMS

1722-1803

Sculptor, ANNE WHITNEY

JOHN WINTHROP

1588-1649

Sculptor, RICHARD S. GREENOUGH

Massachusetts

SAMUEL ADAMS

Managed details of "Boston Tea Party": called "Father of the American Revolution"

> SIGNER, DECL. OF INDEPENDENCE
> Born in Boston, Massachusetts, 1722
> Father, church deacon and owned a brewery
> Samuel studied law to please his father
> Graduated from Harvard College, 1740
> Tax collector of Boston, 1756-1764
> Member, General Court of Mass., 1765-1774
> Member, Continental Congress, 1774-1782
> Opposed all concessions to British Gov't
> Member, Mass. Constitutional Conv., 1779
> President, Mass. State Senate, 1781
> Helped Mass. Conv. ratify U. S. Const., 1788
> Lieutenant Governor, Mass., 1789-1794
> Governor of Massachusetts, 1794-1797
> Died, Boston, 1803; Granary Burial Ground
> Marble statue accepted by Congress, 1876
> Statue located in Statuary Hall

In the achievement of great revolutions which mark and secure the progress of liberty, three kinds of leaders are alike indispensable: the philosopher, who establishes great principles; the statesman, who frames great measures, fills great executive offices, leads popular and legislative assemblies; the politician, without whose marshalling of political forces civil contests must be carried on by mobs and not by parties. Samuel Adams was all three. I know no second instance in history where these three characters have been so wonderfully combined. Yet, what is more wonderful still, Adams was free from the faults which commonly beset each. A profound political philosopher, his feet always touched the ground. He was never led astray by his theory. A statesman, he was without personal ambition. A politician, he was without a wile. . . . The absolute truth and simple honesty of Samuel Adams were unstained.—SENATOR GEORGE FRISBIE HOAR, Massachusetts. *From Congressional Record,* December 19, 1876.

JOHN WINTHROP

He gave all his strength, devotion and fortune to the American colonies

> COLONIZER, 12 TIMES GOVERNOR
> Born near Groton in Suffolk, England, 1588
> Admitted, Trinity College, Cambridge, 1602
> Became Justice of the Peace, Groton, 1609
> Father gave him Manor Lordship, 1619
> A Puritan concerned with religion, morals
> With colony sailed for New World, 1630
> With colony and family settled Boston, 1631
> Gave early success to Mass. Bay Colony
> Governor, Mass. Bay Colony, 12 times
> (1629-34; 1637-40; 1642-44; 1646-49)
> Led United Colonies of New England, 1643
> Foremost planter of Mass. Bay Colony
> He saw the Colony firmly established
> Died, aged by work, anxiety, sorrow, 1649
> Marble statue accepted by Congress, 1876
> Statue located in Hall of Columns

In John Winthrop you see the foremost man of that little company of Englishmen who abandoned wealth, comfort, rank, to found a Christian Church and a Republican State in the wilderness of New England. He was a gentleman of good estate and descent, and of wide and powerful family connection. He was educated at Trinity College, Cambridge, bred to the bar, and had a considerable practice as an attorney of the court of wards and liveries. A large portion of his private papers and letters to his family and friends have been preserved. I know of no other man of his time of whose mental and spiritual life from his childhood up, we have such full particulars. He was a man industrious, modest, wise, brave, generous, affectionate, a lover of home, of kindred and friends, tolerant, religious, moderate, chaste, temperate, self-sacrificing. He had studied the laws of England and thought deeply and clearly upon the principles of civil liberty.—SENATOR GEORGE FRISBIE HOAR, Massachusetts. *From The Congressional Record,* December 19, 1876.

LEWIS CASS

1782-1866

Sculptor, D. C. FRENCH

ZACHARIAH CHANDLER

1813-1879

Sculptor, C. H. NIEHAUS

Michigan

LEWIS CASS

He merited confidence of five presidents who appointed him to high office

SOLDIER, DIPLOMAT, STATESMAN
Born at Exeter, New Hampshire, 1782
Born same year as Webster, Calhoun, Benton
Lewis at Exeter Academy from 1792 to 1799
Taught school in Wilmington, Del., 1799
"Marshal of Ohio," 1807; brig. gen., 1813
Governor, Territory of Michigan, 1813-31
Under Presidents, Madison, Monroe, Adams
Secretary of War, by Pres. Jackson, 1831-36
Sent to France, by Pres. Jackson, 1836-42
Member, U. S. Senate, 1845-1848 (resigned)
Lost candidacy for President, 1848
Member, U. S. Senate, 1849-1857
Sec'y of State, by Pres. Buchanan, 1857-60
Resigned, 1860; died in Detroit, 1866
Marble statue accepted by Congress, 1889
Statue located in Statuary Hall

In responding to the Nation's invitation to the States, that each should place two statues of her illustrious men in Statuary Hall, there was a fitness that the first place should be given by a State to one, if such there be, who more than any other had been identified with her infancy, who had guided her youthful footsteps, who had defended her in war, who had laid down for her rules of conduct, who had brought order out of chaos, who, although separated from her by oceans or called away by public duty, still clung to her as his home. I know of no public man who has filled so many places in the economy of life—teacher, explorer, negotiator of treaties, governor, pioneer, lawyer, legislator, marshal, soldier, diplomat, Secretary of War, Senator, Secretary of State. In all he (Lewis Cass) acquitted himself well. . . . The integrity of his acts is above reproach. — SENATOR THOMAS WITHERELL PALMER, Michigan. *From The Congressional Record*, February 18, 1889.

ZACHARIAH CHANDLER

He helped organize the Republican Party and had important role in maintaining it

PATRIOT, STATESMAN
Born, Bedford, New Hampshire, 1813
Schools: Bedford; Pembroke; Derry Academy
Farm helper; teacher; clerk, Nashua, N. H.
Began dry goods business, Detroit, 1833
Slept in store; lived on $300 a year
Slogan: "Every customer a friend."
Business expanded into a wholesale trade
Friends elected him Mayor of Detroit, 1851
Lost race for Governor on Whig ticket, 1852
Then helped form Republican Party, 1854
In U. S. Senate (after Lewis Cass), 1857-75
Sec'y of Interior (by Pres. Grant), 1875-77
In U. S. Senate, 8 months, 1879, till death
Death followed an Ohio address, 1879
Marble statue unveiled at Capitol, 1913
Statue located in Hall of Columns

Senator Chandler was beloved by his associates and respected by those who disagreed with his political views. The more closely I became connected with him the more I appreciated his great merits. — GENERAL ULYSSES S. GRANT.

Zachariah Chandler was Grant's Secretary of the Interior where his administration is spoken of as "the best in its history." He was the confidant of Lincoln, and probably no man other than Lincoln himself was more steadfast, unyielding, grimly courageous, and unhesitatingly defiant in his opposition to slavery and secession. What this Nation owes to Lincoln for his leadership, partaking of divinity, during the dark days of the sixties, it owes in proportionate measure to Chandler for his lesser but terribly potential work. . . . Every act of Chandler was an act of a staunch and courageous patriot. No taint of dishonesty . . . ever attached to his slightest act.— SENATOR ARTHUR H. VANDENBERG, Michigan. *From the unveiling ceremony,* June 30, 1913.

JEFFERSON DAVIS

1808-1889

Sculptor, AUGUSTUS LUKEMAN

JAMES ZACHARIAH GEORGE

1826-1897

Sculptor, AUGUSTUS LUKEMAN

48

Mississippi

JEFFERSON DAVIS

He was the Political Leader of the Confederate States of America

SOLDIER, STATESMAN
Born in what is now Fairview, Ky., 1808
Jefferson College, Miss.; Transylvania U. Ky.
Graduate, West Point Military Academy, 1828
Served in Black Hawk War, 1830-1831
In 1st Dragoons, 1st lieutenant, 1833
To Miss. plantation, "Brierfield," 1835
Member, U. S. H. of R., 1845-46 (resigned)
With Miss. riflemen in War with Mexico
Member, U. S. Senate, 1847-51 (resigned)
Secretary of War (by Pres. Pierce), 1853-57
Member, U. S. Senate, 1857-1861 (resigned)
Elected President of the Confederacy, 1862
Captured 1865; released 1868; to "Brierfield"
Died, New Orleans, 1889; buried, Richmond
Bronze statue unveiled in Capitol, 1931
Statue located in Statuary Hall

It is fitting that here in this Nation's Capitol, in which he played such a commanding part, this beautiful bronze statue of Jefferson Davis should be placed in tribute to his illustrious achievements and mighty character. How well he adorns it. He is not among strangers; there are his comrades of the South—Lee, Hampton, Wheeler, Stephens, Kirby Smith and James Z. George. With them he scaled the heights of victory and retreated down the slopes of defeat. Over there is Clay, Webster, Benton, Cass and Calhoun, his idol, with whom he served in the Senate of the United States. These men, all, whether divided upon the battle grounds of debate, or united upon the battlefields of war, are entitled to their places here, fixed in the history of a great and reunited country. Jefferson Davis was a devout Christian. . . . He detested hypocrisy and loathed deception. . . . Candor, courage and conviction were the dominating qualities of his matchless character.—SENATOR "PAT" HARRISON, Mississippi. *From unveiling ceremony,* June 2, 1931.

JAMES ZACHARIAH GEORGE

In the aristocratic South he was known as Mississippi's "Great Commoner."

SOLDIER, JURIST, STATESMAN
Born in Monroe County, Georgia, 1826
Moved with mother to Mississippi as a boy
Attended "old field" schools
In Mexican War under Col. Jeff. Davis, 1846
Discharged on account of ill health
Studied law; admitted to bar, 1847
Began practice in Carrollton, Mississippi
Reporter for Miss. Supreme Court, 1854
Captain, colonel, brig. general, Civil War
Resided in Jackson, Mississippi, 1872-87
Chief Justice, State Supreme Court, 1879
Member, U. S. Senate, 1881-97 (till death)
Member, Miss. Constitutional Conv., 1890
Died, Mississippi City, 1897
Bronze statue unveiled in Capitol, 1931
Statue located in Hall of Columns

Not intellect alone made him (Zachariah George) great or gained for him the respect and affection of the people. The character is the man. His character was built on massive lines. Sincerity, the first virtue in everything, was characteristic of him. A matchless integrity marked his every effort. Great principles were his guide. Exalted convictions of duty were the driving force of his nature. Justice was the line, and righteousness the plummet of his life. He was incapable of meanness, and was inflexible in duty. Conscience, intelligent and cultivated, was always a counselor. His opinions were burning convictions. They were alive with moral feeling. The eternal principles of right and wrong were never forgotten. And no bonds of duty were ever worn loosely. In all his actions he endeavored to have them conform to truth, to duty, and to the higher law. . . . Love for humanity was a rooted principle. The welfare of others was his constant solicitude.—SENATOR HUBERT D. STEPHENS, Mississippi. *From unveiling ceremony,* June 2, 1931.

THOMAS H. BENTON

1782-1858

Sculptor, ALEXANDER DOYLE

FRANCIS P. BLAIR

1821-1875

Sculptor, ALEXANDER DOYLE

50

Missouri

THOMAS H. BENTON

He had great influence in making Missouri "The Mother of the West"

STATESMAN, AUTHOR, PIONEER
Born near Hillsboro, Orange Co., N. C., 1782
Ancestors, Revolutionary leaders of 1775
Attended University of North Carolina
With mother to Tenn. estate left by father
Studied law and taught school in Tennessee
Began law practice, Franklin, Tenn., 1806
Member, Tenn. State Legislature, 1809-11
With Jackson, 1812; Lt. Colonel, 1813-15
To St. Louis, Mo.; editor, Missouri Inquirer
In U. S. Senate from Mo., 1821-51 (30 years)
Author, "The Thirty Years View," etc.
Member, U. S. House of R., 1853-55
Promoted Western commerce and fur trade
Died, D. C., 1858; buried, St. Louis, Mo.
Marble statue accepted by House of R., 1899
Statue located in Statuary Hall

Colonel Benton and I became acquainted about forty years ago, and through all that time there was an undeviating friendship between us. . . . He was a man who devoted nearly all his life to the service of this State. . . . To remain in this State and to devote his services to her interests, he refused the highest gifts in the power of the United States Government to bestow. He refused the office of Chief Justice of the United States; he refused being put in nomination for Vice President and other high offices. . . . He was a man of great talents, great energy, and indomitable will. As a father, as a husband, and in all the domestic relations, he was a model. This I know personally. His private and domestic ties were only second to his public duties. He was devoted to the prosperity of this State and to the glory and perpetuity of our Union.—JUDGE WELLS, U. S. Circuit Court. *From address by* HON. JAMES T. LLOYD, M.C., of Missouri, in the House of R., February 4, 1899.

FRANCIS P. BLAIR

Although a Democrat he is credited with having saved Missouri to the Union

SOLDIER, STATESMAN
Born in Lexington, Kentucky, 1821
Family moved to Washington, D. C., 1830
Attended Chapel Hill College, N. C.
Graduate of Princeton College, 1841
Graduate, Transylvania U. Law School, Ky.
Opened law office, St. Louis, Mo., 1843
Member, Mo. contingent U. S. Army, 1846-48
Member, Mo. H. of R. (Democrat), 1852-56
In U. S. House of R. (Republican), 1857-64
(House service made up of broken terms)
Brig. general, 1862; Maj. general, 1863
Member, U. S. Senate (Democrat), 1871-1873
State Insurance Commissioner, 1874
Died in St. Louis, Missouri, 1875
Marble statue accepted by House of R., 1899
Statue located in Hall of Columns

When Francis P. Blair came out of the Army, with his splendid military and civil record, it may be doubted whether there was any official position, however exalted, beyond his reach if he had remained with the Republicans. I have always believed, and do now believe, that by severing his connection with them he probably threw away the Vice Presidency—possibly the Presidency itself. During his long, stormy, and vicissitudinous career he always unhesitatingly did what he thought was right for right's sake, leaving the consequences to take care of themselves. That he was ambitious of political preferment there can be no question; but office had no charms for him if it involved sacrifice of principle or compromise of conscience. . . . His career is without a parallel. Born a Democrat, he served in this House as a Republican, in the Senate as a Democrat, and died, finally, in the political faith of his fathers.—HON. CHAMP CLARK, M.C., of Missouri. *From The Congressional Record*, February 4, 1899.

WILLIAM JENNINGS BRYAN

1860-1925

Sculptor, RUDOLPH EVANS

JULIUS STERLING MORTON

1832-1902

Sculptor, RUDOLPH EVANS

Nebraska

WILLIAM JENNINGS BRYAN

An eloquent, magnetic "Voice of the West" as the 19th Century closed

SOLDIER, ORATOR, STATESMAN
Born in Salem, Illinois, 1860
Graduate, Ill. College, Jacksonville, 1881
Law graduate, Union College, Chicago, 1883
Law practice, Jacksonville; To Nebr., 1887
Delegate, Democratic State Convention, 1888
Member, U. S. House of R., 1891-1895
Gained fame at Demo. Nat'l. Conv., 1896
Lost candidacy for Pres., 1896, 1900, 1908
Nebr. colonel, Spanish-American War, 1898
The Commoner printed, Lincoln, Nebr., 1901
Toured world, 1905-06; author, lecturer
Sec'y of State (by Pres. Wilson), 1913-15
Established home, Miami, Fla., 1921
Died, 1925; buried, Arlington Cemetery
Bronze statue unveiled at Capitol, 1937
Statue located in Statuary Hall

From the pen of one who heard William Jennings Bryan in his first great triumph we have this description: ". . . This young man suddenly appeared, tall, shapely, handsome as a Greek demigod, classic of outline, impassioned of address, thrilling with his tremendous message to the people—appeared like a fairy upon a dull and lifeless stage, and in one moment threw 20,000 human beings into a fever of indescribable exaltation. He stood there, and with a dozen fiery phrases he converted men into fanatics; he changed them as utterly as the wizard changes the toys he plays with on the stage. In all the annals of politics there was never such a scene." But this leader was ahead of his time. The country advanced slowly to the positions upon which this forerunner of progress had taken his earlier stand. One following another, his ideas have been adopted and have proved their worth. Today there is general recognition of a debt of gratitude to William Jennings Bryan.—SEN. EDWARD R. BURKE, Nebraska. *From unveiling ceremony*, April 27, 1937.

J. STERLING MORTON

As "Father of Arbor Day" he encouraged tree planting, especially on the great plains

STATESMAN, ARBOR DAY FOUNDER
Born in Jefferson County, New York, 1832
Family early moved to Detroit, Michigan
Two years at University of Michigan
A.B. Degree, Union College, Schenectady
Homesteaded 160 acres near Nebraska City
This homestead named "Arbor Lodge," 1855
Secretary, Territory of Nebraska, 1858-61
Acting Governor, Territory of Nebr., 1858-59
Helped Nebr. plant 1,000,000 trees, 1872
Sec'y of Agriculture by Cleveland, 1893
Left National office with Pres. Cleveland
Inspired Arbor Day, April 22, for Nebraska
Died at son's home, Lake Forest, Ill., 1902
"Arbor Lodge," Memorial Park given to Nebr.
Bronze statue unveiled at Capitol, 1937
Statue located in Hall of Columns

J. Sterling Morton was a strong and original character. . . . His reputation for mental power, incorruptible integrity of conviction, clear-cut mentality, and moral courage in the maintenance of his views, long since passed beyond the boundaries of this State, and even before he entered the Cabinet of President Cleveland his name was known the wide world over by his most important achievement, the invention and establishment of Arbor Day, which has won for him enduring fame. . . . Mr. Morton's life in Nebraska was dominated for nearly half a century by his example and his precepts in the upbuilding of a strong and useful citizenship in our State and section. He was for all these years essentially a farmer. The practical gospels as to how to raise fine men and women, fine trees, fine apples, fine cattle, fine horses, and fine swine were preached by him in season and out of season through all of our remarkable growth and advance.—HON. KARL STEFAN, M.C., of Nebraska. *From acceptance program*, April 27, 1937.

DANIEL WEBSTER

1782-1852

Sculptor, CARL CONRADS

JOHN STARK

1728-1822

Sculptor, CARL CONRADS

New Hampshire

DANIEL WEBSTER

He ranks with Chief Justice John Marshall as expounder of the Constitution

CONSTITUTIONAL LAWYER
Born in Salisbury, New Hampshire, 1782
Father in Revolution under Gen. Stark
Entered Phillips Exeter Acad., N. H., 1796
In Dartmouth College, 1797-1801 (graduate)
Admitted to the bar, 1805
Practiced law, Portsmouth, N. H., 1807-16
Member, U. S. H. of R. from N. H., 1813-17
Moved to Boston, Massachusetts, 1816
Member, U. S. H. of R., from Mass., 1823-27
Member, U. S. Senate, 1827-41 (resigned)
Sec'y of State, by Pres. Harrison, 1841-43
Member, U. S. Senate, 1845-50 (resigned)
Sec'y of State, by Pres. Fillmore, 1850-52
Died in Marshfield, Mass., 1852
Marble statue accepted by Congress, 1894
Statue located in Statuary Hall

The combination in Daniel Webster's mind and person, of the qualities tending to superiority in each of the three spheres of action— as a lawyer, an orator, and a statesman — marks him as the greatest civilian of the first hundred years of our National existence under our matchless Constitution. . . . He was the great expounder and defender of the American Constitution. There is no military halo around his mighty head; no names of battles tell his fame; but he set forth and explained in living and burning words, as no other did or could, the immortal principles of American govenment, to defend which, navies were built, armies were raised, and our great military chieftains fought and bled and gave up their lives. . . . It is universally conceded that Mr. Webster's intense nationality, which was inherited and was strengthened by the labors of a lifetime in behalf of the American Union, entitles him to the lasting gratitude of his countrymen.—SENATOR WILLIAM E. CHANDLER, New Hampshire. *From The Congressional Record,* December 20, 1894.

JOHN STARK

Surviving two wars, he lived long to enjoy the land he helped to free

SOLDIER, PATRIOT, HERO
Born in what is now Londonderry, Vt., 1728
The father educated his children
Worked at farming, hunting, fishing
Captured by Indians while fur hunting
Fought in French and Indian Wars, 1754-63
Colonel of volunteer army, 1775
Headed N. H. forces at Bunker Hill, 1775
Led Washington's advance, Trenton, 1776
Won the battle of Bennington, 1777
Made major general by Congress, 1786
At close of war returned to N. H. home
Took up pursuit of agriculture
Outlived all Rev. generals save Gen. Sumter
Died, 1822 (45 years after Bennington)
Marble statue accepted by Congress, 1894
Statue located in Court Vestibule

General Stark impressed everyone with his self confidence, his self-possession in times of difficulty or danger, his capacity to command, his power to execute, and his courage at all times. His character in private and public life is without a stain. Though stern and unrelenting when duty called or honor was involved he was open and frank in his manners. He was always kind to the needy and hospitable to all, especially to his comrades in arms. His integrity was unquestioned, his honor never doubted. His patriotism was pure and perennial. He said, "The cause of my Country appears the noblest for which man ever contended, and no measures should be neglected or sacrifices withheld which will support it to a favorable result. In such a cause we may even despise death itself. I am most happy when I can do my Country the greatest service."—HON. HENRY MOORE BAKER, M.C. of New Hampshire. *From The Congressional Record,* December 20, 1894.

RICHARD STOCKTON

1730-1781

Sculptor, H. K. BROWN

GENERAL PHILIP KEARNY

1814-1862

Sculptor, H. K. BROWN

New Jersey

RICHARD STOCKTON

Occupied high point of half dozen successive generations of distinguished Stocktons

SIGNER, DECL. OF INDEPENDENCE
Born in Princeton, New Jersey, 1730
Family estate, "Morven" in heart of Princeton
Early education at Nottingham, Maryland
Graduate, Princeton College, N. J., 1748
Studied law; became licensed attorney, 1754
Chief financial adviser to his Alma Mater
Visited England, 1766; returned to "Morven"
Justice, New Jersey Supreme Court, 1774
Member, Continental Congress, 1776
Ordered to visit Northern Army, 1776
Captured by loyalists; N. Y. imprisonment
Formal remonstrance from Congress, 1777
Released; "Morven" pillaged; fortune gone
Shattered health; died at Princeton, 1781
Marble statue accepted by Congress, 1888
Statue located in Statuary Hall

As a farmer, lawyer, judge, Member of Congress, son, husband, father and friend, he was a model. The well rounded symmetry of his character always reminded me of Washington whose friendship he enjoyed. Except that Stockton's life and character had no military tinge there was a striking resemblance between these two men. They were both perfect gentlemen of the antique world; courteous, dignified, methodical, never forgetting themselves, and in justice let me say, never forgetting anyone else whom they should remember.... I can picture Washington at Mt. Vernon, Stockton at Morven, and I can believe this New Jersey gentleman had no greater pride than in recalling his stainless and distinguished line of ancestry, unless Providence had kindly lifted for him the veil of the future that he might behold his son, his grandson, and his great grandson occupying seats in the Senate ... as regularly as if they were a Stockton heirloom.—HON. WILLIAM WALTER PHELPS, M.C. of New Jersey. *From The Congressional Record,* August 21, 1888.

GENERAL PHILIP KEARNY

A "perfect soldier" who followed the path of glory to the grave

"THE PERFECT SOLDIER"
Born in New York, 1814; wealthy family
Mother died, 1823; boyhood with grandfather
Graduate, Columbia College, 1833; Europe
Grandfather opposed West Point and war
Grandfather left Philip $1,000,000 estate
Philip in U.S. Army as 2nd lieutenant, 1835
On frontier 2 years; Cavalry tactics, France
In Algiers, 1840; With Gen. Scott, 1848
Shattered left arm in Mexican battle
Resigned, 1851; took trip around world
Maj. general, Civil War; 12 engagements
Killed at Chantilly, Va. Sept. 1, 1862
Buried at Trinity Churchyard, New York
Reburied, Arlington National Cemetery, 1912
Bronze statue accepted by Congress, 1888
Statue located in Hall of Columns

Brave as a lion, tender as a woman, his portrait remains the beau ideal of the soldier, and the picture of that slim, handsome figure riding all alone to its death at Chantilly, with his bridle in his teeth and his only remaining arm waving his sword, goes down in history as symbolic of the character and conduct of this gallant leader.... His intensity of nature generally controlled him and brought with it all its natural advantages and disadvantages. Had this fierce enthusiasm been for an unworthy object, it would have been inexcusable and baneful. Fortunately, it was almost always directed to a noble and unselfish end. ... May our Country never lack the unselfish wisdom in her later councils which Richard Stockton gave in her earliest, and may she never lack in the execution of them the self-devotion which made Philip Kearny, for his Country's sake, ride to death as to a festival. —HON. WILLIAM W. PHELPS, M.C. of *New Jersey. From The Congressional Record,* August 21, 1888.

ROBERT R. LIVINGSTON

1746-1813

Sculptor, ERASTUS DOW PALMER

GEORGE CLINTON

1739-1812

Sculptor, H. K. BROWN

New York

ROBERT R. LIVINGSTON

The diplomacy of Chancelor Livingston brought about the purchase of Louisiana

> JURIST, DIPLOMAT, STATESMAN
> Born in New York City, 1746
> Graduate, Kings College, now Columbia, 1765
> Admitted to bar, 1773; In Cont'l. Cong, 1776
> On drafting Committee for Dec'l. of Ind.
> Secretary of Foreign Affairs, 1781
> Chancellor, New York State, 1771-1801
> Administered oath to Pres. Washington, 1789
> Minister to France by Jefferson, 1801-1805
> Livingston diplomacy purchased Louisiana
> Became partner of Robert Fulton in Paris
> Boat *Clermont* named for Livingston mansion
> Steam navigation owes much to Livingston
> First Pres. American Academy of Fine Arts
> Died at Clermont, New York, 1813
> Bronze statue placed in Capitol, 1874
> Statue located in Statuary Hall

It was argued by Robert R. Livingston and others that though they were friends to the measures themselves (that the Colonies be absolved from all obedience to the British crown, and that all political connection between them and the State of Great Britain ought to be totally dissolved) and saw the impossibility that we should ever again be united with Great Britain, yet they were against adopting them at this time: that the conduct we had formerly observed was wise and proper now, of deferring to take any capital step till the voice of the people drove us into it: that they were our power and without them our declarations could not be carried into effect: that the people of the middle colonies were not yet ripe for bidding adieu to British connections, but that they were fast ripening, and in a short time would join in the general voice of America.—THOMAS JEFFERSON, Member, Continental Congress, Virginia. *From Journals of the Continental Congress,* June 7, 1776.

GEORGE CLINTON

He was a strong man among giants—teammate of Jefferson and Madison

> VICE PRESIDENT OF THE U. S.
> Born in Little Britain, Ulster Co., N. Y., 1739
> Not averse to study but liked exciting life
> Ran away from home to fight French, 1755
> Fought under his father at Fort Frontenac
> Admitted to the bar in his native county
> Member, New York State Assembly, 1768
> Delegate, 2nd Continental Congress, 1775
> Brigadier general, N. Y. militia, 1777
> First Governor of New York, 1777-1795
> Pres. N. Y. Conv. ratifying U. S. Const.
> Elected Governor again, 1801-1804
> V. P. for Jefferson, 1804; for Madison, 1808
> Died, D. C., 1812; buried, Congressional Cem.
> Reburied, Kingston, New York, 1908
> Bronze statue placed in Capitol, 1873
> Statue located in Vestibule S. of Rotunda

Gentlemen, upon me devolves the painful duty of announcing to the Senate the death of our venerable fellow-citizen, George Clinton, Vice President of the United States. By this afflictive dispensation of Divine Providence the Senate is deprived of a President rendered dear to each of its Members by the dignity and impartiality with which he has so long presided over their deliberations; and the nation bereaved of one of the brightest luminaries of its glorious Revolutions.—SENATOR WILLIAM H. CRAWFORD, Georgia. President pro tempore of the Senate. April 20, 1812.

Resolved unanimously, that, from an unfeigned respect to the late George Clinton, Vice President of the United States, and President of the Senate, the Chair of the President of the Senate be shrouded with black during the present session; and . . . the Members of the Senate will go into mourning and wear a black crape round the left arm for thirty days. SENATE RESOLUTION. *From Congressional Globe,* April 21, 1812.

ZEBULON BAIRD VANCE

1830-1894

Sculptor, GUTZON BORGLUM

CHARLES BRANTLEY AYCOCK

1859-1912

Sculptor, CHARLES KECK

North Carolina

ZEBULON BAIRD VANCE

His divided loyalty, reunited after war, increased in fervor for the Union.

SOLDIER, STATESMAN
Born near Asheville, North Carolina, 1830
Received good education at village school
Attended Washington College, Tennessee
Attended University of N. C. at Chapel Hill
Admitted to bar; elected Co. Attorney, 1852
Member, U. S. House of R. at 28 (1858-61)
Volunteered for war service, 1861
Captain then colonel, N. C. State troops
Governor, North Carolina, 1862-1866
Lost election to U. S. Senate, 1872
Again Governor of North Carolina, 1876-78
Member, U. S. Senate, 1879-1894 (till death)
Died, D. C., 1894; services, Senate Chamber
Burial, Riverside Cemetery, Asheville, N. C.
Bronze statue accepted by Congress, 1916
Statue located in Statuary Hall

Forty-six years ago I began to consider the life of Zebulon B. Vance. I found then that the lode star of his life was truth; that the compass by which he sailed his bark was consecrated to present duty; that his character contained something more than knowledge, industry, and eloquence; that it had wrapped up within it that most priceless jewel of humanity—influence—and that that influence was never used in an unworthy cause nor for the purpose of self-aggrandizement. As he passed from the keeping of North Carolina into the keeping of the Republic, he sailed an unvarying course toward truth and honor and justice. . . . His courage in war, his patriotism in peace, his unselfish devotion to the rights of man are a memory which sweetens the sleep of every North Carolinian, strengthens the arm of every American and heartens the hope of every young man who wants to do right for right's sake. — HON. THOMAS R. MARSHALL, Vice President. *From acceptance proceedings,* June 22, 1916.

CHARLES BRANTLEY AYCOCK

He was a friend of public education and as Governor officially sponsored it

LAWYER, GOVERNOR, EDUCATOR
Born, Wayne Co. (near Fremont) N. C., 1859
Schools: Nahunta; Wilson; Kingston (N. C.)
Graduate, University of N. C., 1880
Began law practice, Goldsboro, N. C., 1881
Sup. Public Instruction, Wayne Co., 1881
U. S. Attorney, Eastern Dist. N. C., 1893-97
Governor of North Carolina, 1901-1905
Back to law practice at Goldsboro, 1905
Moved to Raleigh North Carolina, 1909
Continued law practice in Raleigh
Continued great work for education
Died in Birmingham, Alabama, 1912
Addressing Ala. Educational Association
Buried in Raleigh, North Carolina
Bronze statue unveiled at Capitol, 1932
Statue located in Hall of Columns

This statue of Governor Aycock will be a reminder that heroes of victories in the cause of education deserve to rank beside the heroes of national defense, statesmanship, and pioneering enterprise. . . UNITED STATES OFFICE OF EDUCATION. *From letter read at unveiling ceremony,* May 10, 1932.

Governor Aycock did for education in North Carolina what Horace Mann did for it in Massachusetts, and like Horace Mann, he rendered a never-ending service to the schools of the Nation. The greatest need in the educational crisis of today is an educational governor of the type of Governor Aycock in every State in the Union—one who sets forth the great value of education in our democracy and one who places the interests of childhood above the need for fine roads and that of extensive public improvements. Education in this Nation craves friends of his type in every community. — THE NATIONAL EDUCATION ASSOCIATION. *From letter read at unveiling ceremony,* May 10, 1932.

WILLIAM ALLEN

1803-1879

Sculptor, C. H. NIEHAUS

JAMES A. GARFIELD

1831-1881

Sculptor, C. H. NIEHAUS

Ohio

WILLIAM ALLEN

He was elected Governor at 71 after 25 years without political office

GOVERNOR, STATESMAN
Born, Edenton, North Carolina, 1803
Early schooling, Lynchburg, Virginia
Moved to Chillicothe, Ohio, 1819
Studied law in office of Edward King
Admitted to bar, 1827; was King's partner
Member, U. S. House of R., 1833-1835
Member, U. S. Senate, 1837-1849
Retired to estate near Chillicothe, Ohio
Lived here, "Fruit Hill" 25 years, 1849-74
During Civil War was anti-war Democrat
Also critic of Lincoln Administration
Became Governor of Ohio, 1874-1876
Back to "Fruit Hill" and agriculture
Died at home, 1879; buried, Chillicothe
Marble statue placed in Capitol, 1888
Statue located in Statuary Hall

Riding the circuit, in accordance with frontier custom, William Allen soon became a noted local figure; his large stature and commanding presence, his fluency of speech and skill in debate won for him a reputation throughout the state... He was an ardent expansionist and a frequent declaimer on the Senate floor for the rights of the United States in Oregon, and for the annexation of Texas... He voiced at all times what he believed to be aspirations and ideals of the West. His essential honesty was never questioned. — DICTIONARY OF AMER. BIOGRAPHY.

William Allen was born in the State of Nathaniel Macon and delivered sentiments worthy of the school of that great patriot, and delivered in a style to adorn his station. He had the elevated and constitutional view of the subject, and showed himself to be the defender of the compromises on which this Union was founded. — SENATOR THOMAS HART BENTON, Missouri. *From The Congressional Globe,* September 26, 1837.

JAMES A. GARFIELD

America's second martyred President after years of distinguished public service

PRESIDENT OF THE UNITED STATES
Born in Orange, Ohio, 1831
To District school three months each year
Driver and helmsman on Ohio Canal, 1848
Attended Eclectic Institute, Ohio, 1851-54
Graduate, Williams College, Mass., 1858
Member, Ohio State Senate, 1859
President, Hiram College, Ohio, 1857-61
Admitted to bar, 1860; Lt. colonel, 1861
Brig. general, 1862; major general, 1863
U. S. House of R., 1863-1880 (resigned)
Elected to U. S. Senate, 1880 (declined)
Inaugurated President, March 4, 1881
Shot in Washington, D. C., July 2, 1881
Died, Sept. 19, 1881; buried, Cleveland, O.
Marble statue accepted by Congress, 1886
Statue located in Capitol Rotunda

In principle James A. Garfield was in every sense a patriot. No narrow limit confined his allegiance, but the whole country was the object of his love. He did not favor any section, but freely extended the bounties of Government to every part. He was a lover of liberty, of freedom in its broadest sense, not only of the person, but of thought and of speech. Though a member of the Disciple Church, he was Catholic in his charity for all Christian denominations... He was a strict guardian of the public faith, pledged either to a citizen, a soldier, or a creditor... A striking example himself of the benefits of education, he favored every measure to extend and enlarge the scope of both State and National aid to education. He was a Republican, not in the narrow sense of personal advantage, but because he believed that party could best advance the honor and prosperity of our whole country, and of every part of it.—SENATOR JOHN SHERMAN, Ohio. *From The Congressional Record,* January 5, 1886.

SEQUOYA

1770-1844

Sculptors, VINNIE REAM AND G. J. ZOLNAY

WILL ROGERS

1879-1935

Sculptor, JO DAVIDSON

Oklahoma

SEQUOYA

Through invention of the Cherokee alphabet he gave his people a written language

    PHILSOPHER, INVENTOR, CHIEF
    Disputed birthplace—probably Georgia, 1770
    Cherokee Indian; no educational advantages
    Never learned to read or write English
    Invented a phonetic alphabet, 85 symbols
    Began alphabet, 1809; completed it, 1821
    Moved West with other members of his tribe
    Cherokees settled Indian Territory in 1823
    Was voted silver medal by his tribe, 1824
    Became fine silversmith; man of intellect
    Represented Cherokees in Washington, 1828
    Congress gave $500.00 for his benefit
    Printed first newspaper in Indian language
    Parts of Bible printed with his alphabet
    Died, near San Bernardino, Calif. 1844 (?)
    Bronze statue unveiled in Capitol, 1917
    Statue located in Statuary Hall.

The placing of a statue of Sequoya in Statuary Hall is a very fitting and appropriate recognition of the Indian race. His fame rests upon his achievement in inventing an alphabet for the Cherokee Indian Nation. . . Like Whitney, Howe, McCormick, Edison, and practically all other inventors, Sequoya secceeded in his invention by industry, perseverance, and concentration. After accomplishing this great work, he then endeared himself to his people through his devotion to service in teaching them how to read and write. The General Council of the Cherokee Nation passed a resolution awarding Sequoya a silver medal as a token of their gratitude for his great services. . . Sequoya, without education, without intellectual training, and during his life having been associated with an unlettered people—with all these handicaps—he still made for himself a place in the history of our Nation.—HON. DICK THOMPSON MORGAN, *M.C. of Oklahoma. From unveiling ceremony,* June 6, 1917.

WILL ROGERS

He represents in high degree the kindly humor and shrewd commonsense of the frontier

    PHILOSOPHER, HUMORIST, WRITER
    Born near Oologah, Indian Territory, 1879
    Will grew up on the simple frontier
    He learned to look for the best in people
    Schools: Willie Hassell in Neosho, Mo.
    Kemper Military Academy in Boonville, Mo.
    Cherokee Indian descent; worked as cowboy
    Beloved star of stage, screen and radio
    Foremost humorist of his time
    Popular columnist; world traveler
    Well known author of several books
    Claremore, Oklahoma became his home town
    Last journey, world plane trip, Wiley Post
    Killed. Post plane crashed, Alaska, 1935
    Body removed to Claremore for burial
    Bronze statue unveiled in Capitol, 1939
    Statue located in House Connection

Will Rogers was the big brother of the world whose wholesome humor always boosted the fellow who needed a lift. . . . His humor took the sting out of political strife and poured oil on the troubled waters of international controversies. His humor was the safety valve for American life. The high tension of our fast-moving life found release of pressure in his wit and wisdom. He never used sarcasm nor cynicism. He never destroyed an ideal, crushed an ambition, withered a hope, or disillusioned a dreamer; but instead he encouraged, he cheered, he inspired. . . His charity was unlimited. He accumulated a fortune but gave away more than he kept. He tithed by keeping one-tenth and giving away nine. . . His life gave people faith in humanity and confidence in one another. Few men become ideals while they still live. But just as the flag is more than a piece of colored bunting, so also was Will Rogers more than a mere man. He was an ideal.—SENATOR JOSHUA B. LEE, Oklahoma. *From unveiling ceremony,* June 6, 1939.

REVEREND JASON LEE

1803-1845

Sculptor, GIFFORD MACGREGOR PROCTOR

DR. JOHN MCLOUGHLIN

1784-1857

Sculptor, GIFFORD MACGREGOR PROCTOR

Oregon

REVEREND JASON LEE

He was leader and founder of American colonization and civilization in Oregon

MISSIONARY, SEER, COLONIZER
Born in Vermont (now part of Quebec) 1803
Last of 15 children; father died, 1806
Jason was self-supporting at 13 years old
To village school, now Stanstead, Quebec
Was converted by Wesleyan Missionary, 1826
Attended Methodist Academy, Mass., 1829
Became teacher, preacher, Stanstead, Quebec
West to Oregon with cavalcade, April, 1834
Mission near Salem; met Dr. McLoughlin
Back to N. Y. to interest Congress, 1838
Brought a party of 51 West by boat, 1840
This new Mission later became Willamette U.
Back to Stantsead to live with sister, 1843
Died, Stanstead, 1845; reburied, Salem, 1906
Bronze statue unveiled in Capitol, 1953
Statue located in Statuary Hall

Jason Lee was a large, athletic young man, six feet and three inches in height, with a fully developed frame and a constitution like iron. His piety was deep and uniform, and his life, in a very uncommon degree, pure and exemplary. In those days of extensive and powerful revivals they regarded him as a righteous man whose prayers availed much. — BISHOP OSMON C. BAKER, Classmate of Jason Lee.

The precious jewel of a Commonwealth, the one thing above all others which it should treasure, is the memory of those grand and self-sacrificing men and women who laid the foundations of its greatness and prosperity. One of these treasured memories is the life and work of Jason Lee, the founder of American civilization in Oregon... Lee combined the fervor of a Missionary, the foresight of a seer, and the patriotism of a loyal citizen. — THOMAS A. MCBRIDE, Justice, Oregon State Supreme Court. *From unveiling ceremony*, February 16, 1953.

DR. JOHN McLOUGHLIN

Though agent for a British Corporation he encouraged Oregon settlement by Americans

COLONIZER, EMPIRE BUILDER
Born at Riviere du Loup, Quebec, 1784
At age of 14 began medical apprenticeship
Admitted to practice of medicine at 19
With North West Co. fur traders, 1803-14
Became "wintering partner" of Co., 1814
North West Co. joined Hudson's Bay, 1821
Hudson's Bay claimed all west of Rockies
McLoughlin appointed head of region, 1824
Became authority with this British Company
Welcomed Jason Lee and Missionaries, 1834
Welcomed first colonizing settlers, 1843
Resigned position, 1845; home, Oregon City
Moved toward American citizenship, 1849
Died at his home in Oregon City, 1857
Bronze statue unveiled in Capitol, 1953
Statue located in House Connection

Dr. McLoughlin, local representative of the Hudson's Bay Company, constituted in his person the sole business and, since the Hudson's Bay Company was British, the sole governmental authority in the entire Columbia River region from the time of his appointment in 1824 until shortly before the time of his resignation, 1845. It was under his mild and just paternalistic rule that the region grew from a wilderness of savages to a settled country, learned to govern itself and built schools and churches, and passed peacefully from British rule to American territorial status... Dr. McLoughlin was noted for the welcome he gave to missionaries of all faiths, and the substantial help he afforded to them and to the farmers whose coming spelled ruin to the business of the Hudson's Bay Company's fur business... One of the glories of Dr. McLoughlin's career was his hearty welcome of the Reverend Jason Lee, Methodist Missionary, and his companions in 1834.— HON. SAM COON, M. C. of Oregon. *From The Congressional Record*, February 16, 1953.

ROBERT FULTON

1765-1815

Sculptor, HOWARD ROBERTS

JOHN PETER GABRIEL MUHLENBERG

1746-1807

Sculptor, BLANCHE NEVIN

Pennsylvania

ROBERT FULTON

His invention bound together this vast Country by power transportation

> ARTIST, CIVIL ENGINEER, INVENTOR
> Born in Little Britain, Pennsylvania, 1765
> Early education slight; private school, 1773
> Showed genius for drawing and invention
> Sold gun drawings; expert gunsmith
> Artist in Philadelphia, 1782; there 4 years
> To London in poor health, 1786; there 20 yrs.
> Left art for engineering projects, invention
> Increased interest in mechanical equipment
> Worked on submarine mines and torpedoes
> Met Robert R. Livingston in France
> Became partners, making first steamboat
> Fulton's "Clermont" plied the Hudson, 1807
> He finally headed steamboat industry
> Died, N. Y. City, 1815; buried at Trinity
> Marble statue placed in Capitol, 1889
> Statue located in Statuary Hall

Fulton, by his successful application of steam to purposes of water navigation, as by the wand of a magician, revolutionized the commerce and trade of his day and of the world. By experiments in naval torpedo warfare he pioneered the way for the wholesale destruction of navies, to remedy and ward off which great governments are spending countless sums. The immense streams of the country were made tributary to the Nation's greatness. Old ocean rolled his waves submissive to the paddle of the steamer, and found a master despite adverse winds. Today, rivers, bays, gulfs and oceans the world over are dotted with innumerable argosies propelled by steam-moving monuments bearing unmistakable testimony to the triumph of mind over matter, to its domination over the forces of nature, to the unflagging zeal, to the skill, and to the genius of Robert Fulton. This genuis of Fulton's embraces empires, co-extensive with the known world.—HON. DANIEL ERMENTROUT, M.C. of Pa. *From The Congressional Record,* February 28, 1889.

GENERAL J. P. G. MUHLENBERG

Outstanding Revolutionary patriot of six Muhlenbergs who served 17 U.S. Congresses

> SOLDIER, MINISTER, STATESMAN
> Born at Trappe, Pennsylvania, 1746
> Father, Lutheran Minister in Philadelphia
> To Philadelphia Academy, now Uni. of Pa.
> To Halle, Germany, study for Ministry, 1763
> Lutheran pastor, America, 1766, Pa., Va., N.J.
> From Woodstock, Va. pulpit to Pa. militia
> Brig. general, 1777; major general, 1783
> With Washington—Brandywine to Yorktown
> V. Pres. Pa. Executive Council, 1785-1787
> Member, Pa. Constitutional Convention, 1790
> U.S. House of R., 1789-91; 1793-95; 1799-1801
> Member, U.S. Senate, 1801 (resigned)
> Revenue job by Pres. Jefferson, 1801, Pa.
> Died near Philadelphia, 1807; buried, Trappe
> Marble statue placed in Capitol, 1889
> Statue located, vestibule S. of Rotunda

The voice of John Peter Muhlenberg in the Virginia House of Burgesses and the Committee of Safety was but that of the Pennsylvania German missionary speaking for and leading the Pennsylvania Germans of the Shenandoah. He went there in 1772, was there but two years as a pastor, and then from that time on he was wherever duty called, rendering his services to the whole country. Washington found in him not only a consummate officer but a trustworthy adviser. . . The struggle over, liberty achieved, covered with honors of war, he returned to his native state, and again his counsel and his voice were given to mold her government and the Nation's laws. . . He was of tall stature, robust and animated. . . In his character he was open, amiable, and without arrogance. But if there was one trait which controlled his life, his political principles and his conduct, and which stamped his inner being, it was a love of Liberty. — HON. DANIEL ERMENTROUT, M.C. of Pennsylvania. *From The Congressional Record,* February 28, 1889.

ROGER WILLIAMS

1604-1683

Sculptor, FRANKLIN SIMMONS

NATHANIEL GREENE

1742-1786

Sculptor, H. K. BROWN

Rhode Island

ROGER WILLIAMS

He colonized Rhode Island, befriended the Indians, and fathered religious liberty

    COLONIZER, "GODLY MINISTER"
Born, London, 1604 (?); son of merchant
Graduate, Pembroke Coll., Cambridge, 1627
Cambridge prepared him for the Church
Answered New England call; sailed, 1630
Welcomed at Mass. Bay as "a godly minister"
Banished for "dangerous opinions", 1635
Helped and loved by friendly Indians
Founded Rhode Island at Providence, 1636
Made peace with Indians during Pequot War
Got charter for Providence Plantation, 1644
Religious liberty—"The Rhode Island Way"
King Philip's War; peace with Indians gone
Died, grieving over Indian Wars, 1683 (?)
Like Moses, "No man knoweth his sepulcher"
Marble statue accepted by Congress, 1872
Statue located in Statuary Hall

Rhode Island would have been untrue to her antecedents had she failed to name her first citizen, Roger Williams, for a place in our National Gallery of Statues because of his prominence in our history. But it is not because he was the founder of a city, nor because he planted a Colony, from the loins of which has sprung a vigorous State, that Rhode Island has resolved to set up his statue in the Capitol of the Nation; but she has accorded him the honor because he successfully vindicated the right of private judgment in matters of conscience, and effected a moral and political revolution in all governments of the civilized world... The merit of Williams in announcing and maintaining this then strange and heretical doctrine is therefore to be estimated with reference to the adverse tendencies and opinions of the period. He alone brought the great work of the Reformation to its last grand stage of development.— SENATOR WILLIAM SPRAGUE, Rhode Island. *From The Congressional Record,* January 9, 1872.

NATHANIEL GREENE

He dealt staggering blows to British in southern colonies during the Revolution

    REVOLUTIONARY GENERAL
Born at Potowomut, Rhode Island, 1742
Good student; ability in mathematics
Deputy, General Assembly, 1770-72; 1775
Brig. general, 1775; maj. general, 1776
Quartermaster General, by Congress, 1778
Resigned, word of Washington, Aug. 1780
Succeeded General Gates, October, 1780
"Great tact and ability in handling men"
Used own fortune for suffering soldiers
Hailed by many as "Savior of the South"
Georgia gave him plantation near Savannah
Two homes: Rhode Island and Georgia, 1783
Home: "Mulberry Grove", Savannah, 1785
Died at home, 1786; buried in Savannah
Marble statue accepted by Congress, 1870
Statue located in vestibule N. of Rotunda

You have conducted the various duties of the office of Quartermaster General with capacity and diligence, entirely to my satisfaction and, as far as I have had opportunity of knowing, with the strictest integrity. When you were prevailed upon to undertake the office in March, 1778, it was in great disorder and confusion, and by extraordinary exertions you so arranged it as to enable the Army to take the field the moment it was necessary, and to move with rapidity after the enemy when they left Philadelphia. From that period to the present time your exertions have been equally great. They have appeared to me to be the result of system, and to have been well calculated to promote the interests and honor of your Country. In fine, I cannot but add that the States have had in you, in my opinion, an able, upright, and diligent servant.— GENERAL WASHINGTON'S LETTER TO NATHANIEL GREENE *upon Greene's retirement from the office of Quartermaster General,* August 15, 1780.

JOHN C. CALHOUN

1782-1850

Sculptor, F. W. RUCKSTULL

WADE HAMPTON

1818-1902

Sculptor, F. W. RUCKSTULL

South Carolina

JOHN C. CALHOUN

He was the recognized brainy leader of the southern school of constitutionalists

CONSTITUTIONAL LAWYER
Born in Abbeville Co. South Carolina, 1782
John's ancestors were Revolutionary leaders
Early education in country schools of S. C.
Graduated from Yale with merit, 1804
Studied law in Conn. and Charleston, S. C.
Member S. Carolina House of R., 1808-09
In U. S. House of R., 1811-17 (resigned)
Sec'y of War, by Pres. Monroe, 1817-1825
Vice Pres. of the U. S., 1825-32 (resigned)
Member, U. S. Senate, 1832-43 (resigned)
Sec'y of State, by Pres. Tyler, 1844-45
Declined English mission by Pres. Polk
Member, U. S. Senate, 1845-50 (till death)
Died, Washington, D. C., 1850; buried, S. C.
Marble statue unveiled in Capitol, 1910
Statue located in Statuary Hall

Mr. Calhoun was plain in manner, some thought too austere, but to those who came in close contact with him his personality was most charming and engaging. He coveted no title, and was known to all his neighbors and friends as "Mr. Calhoun". . . His life was marked by serious, sincere convictions of his public responsibilities. He was in no sense of the word a time-server. His hold upon the people of his own state was not obtained by personal clamor or by any ordinary political methods. He led public thought by logical appeals to reason and by the purity and honesty of his public and private life. In all his public acts he was above reproach and no whisper of improper motives or selfish ambition ever touched his name or fame. He was an ardent lover of the Union and its institutions, only pleading in his manly and outspoken way for a strict observance and just interpretation of the Constitutional and binding obligations of our federal compact.— Hon. W. L. Mauldin, Statue Commission. *From unveiling ceremonies,* March 12, 1910.

WADE HAMPTON

He combined loyalties to the old south and to the new south and also to the Union

SOLDIER, STATESMAN, PLANTER
Born in Charleston, South Carolina, 1818
Early schooling with private instructors
Grandfather owner of 3,000 slaves, 1830
Graduate, S. C. Coll., (now U. of S. C.) 1837
Studied law but never practiced
Member, S. C. State Senate, 1858-1862
Colonel in Confederate Army, 1861
Raised and commanded "Hampton's Legion"
Brigadier general of Cavalry, 1862
Major general, Confederate Army, 1863
Lieutenant general, Confederate Army, 1865
Governor of South Carolina, 1876-1879
Member, U. S. Senate, 1879-1891
Died in Columbia, S. C., 1902
Marble statue unveiled in Capitol, 1929
Statue located in House Connection

It was because the people of South Carolina loved Wade Hampton and still revere his memory, as they have never loved nor revered the memory of any other man, that they have chosen him for this great honor, and . . . is not the love of a people the best criterion by which human greatness can be judged, provided that love is inspired by unselfish and patriotic service to State and Country? . . . And let this be clearly understood. It is not only on account of Wade Hampton's war record, nor even the great part he played in redeeming South Carolina in the days of reconstruction, but also on account of the example of loyalty to a reunited country which he later, as a Senator of the United States, set for the people of the South to follow, and the patriotic sentiments he so often expressed under the Dome of this Capitol which have caused the people of his State to place his statue in this Hall.—Hon. Duncan C. Heyward, former Governor of South Carolina. *From unveiling ceremonies,* June 10, 1929.

73

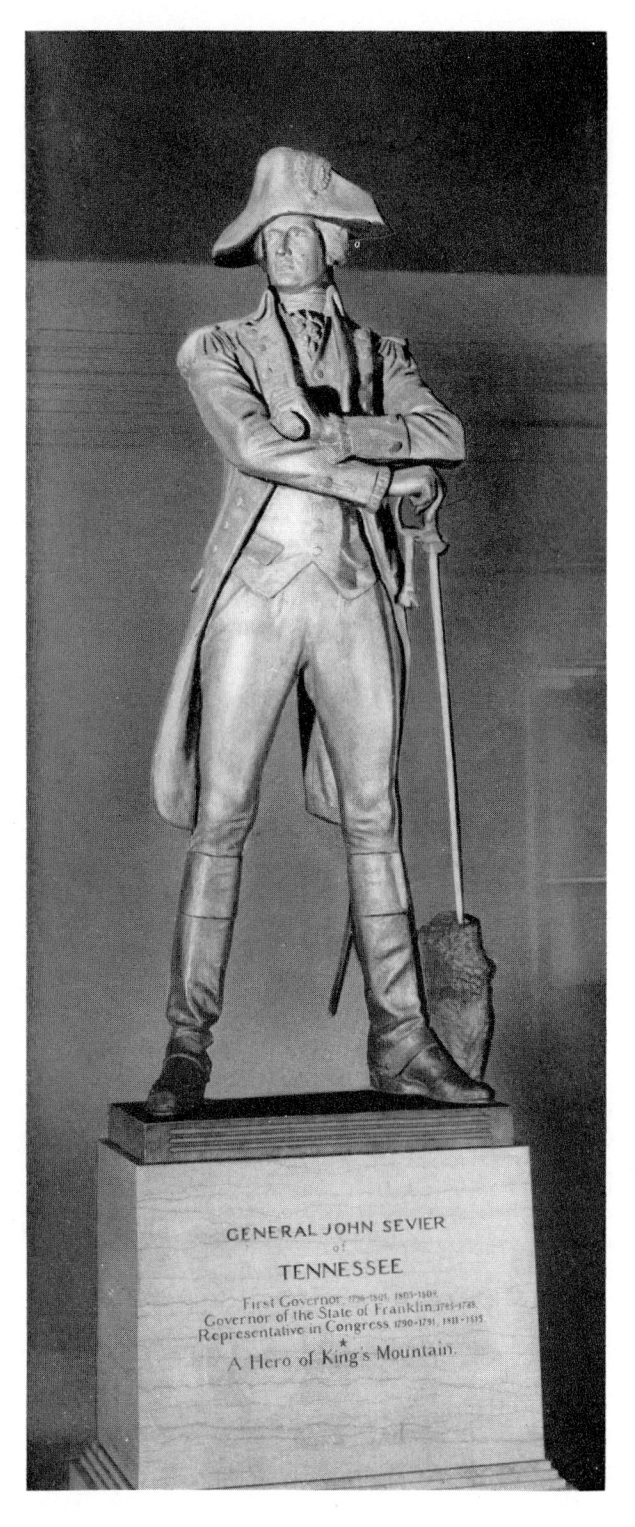

GENERAL JOHN SEVIER

1745-1815

Sculptors, BELLE KINNEY AND L. F. SCHOLZ

GENERAL ANDREW JACKSON

1767-1845

Sculptors, BELLE KINNEY AND L. F. SCHOLZ

Tennessee

JOHN SEVIER

He was a brilliant frontier leader both in war and peace

> PIONEER, SOLDIER, STATESMAN
> Born in Rockingham County, Virginia, 1745
> Early schooling at Fredericksburg, Virginia
> Moved to what is now N.E. Tennessee, 1773
> Captain, Colonial Militia, 1773-1774
> County Clerk and District Judge, 1777-1780
> Prominent in Battle of Kings Mountain, 1780
> With General Greene in S. C., 1781
> Led fight against Chickamaugas, 1782
> Gov. "Proclaimed State of Franklin," 1785-88
> Member, U. S. House of R., 1789-91
> Brigadier general of militia, 1791
> Governor of Tenn., 1796-1801, 1803-1809
> Member, U. S. House of R., 1811, till death
> Died, Ala, 1815; reburied, Knoxville, 1855
> Bronze statue unveiled in Capitol, 1931
> Statue located in Statuary Hall

John Sevier's vigorous and effective personality and constructive leadership have unquestionably been dominating factors in the glorious history of the Commonwealth of which he was first governor. In paying tribute to this statesman let me quote what a great American of later day—President Roosevelt —said of him, "Sevier was a gentleman of birth and breeding... To the end of his days he was an interested and intelligent observer of men and things both in America and Europe. He corresponded on intimate and equal terms with Madison, Franklin, and others of our most polished statesmen... Sevier was a very handsome man, reputed during his life the very handsomest in Tennessee. He was tall, fair skinned, blue eyed, brown haired, of slender build, with erect, military carriage, and commanding bearing... From his French forefathers he had inherited a gay, pleasure-loving temperament that made him the most charming of companions.—HON. F. TRUBEE DAVISON, Assistant Secretary of War. *From unveiling ceremony*, April 19, 1931.

ANDREW JACKSON

His victory at New Orleans helped to avoid a third war with Great Britain

> PRESIDENT OF THE UNITED STATES
> Born in Carolina Waxhaw settlement, 1767
> In Revolutionary Army at 13; orphan at 14
> Began law practice, McLeanville, N. C., 1787
> To Tenn. 1788; became a pioneer leader
> Member, U. S. House of R. 1796 (3 months)
> Member, U. S. Senate, 1797 (resigned, 1798)
> Member, Tenn. Supreme Court, 1798-1804
> Moved to Hermitage near Nashville
> Won great renown in Creek War, 1813-1814
> Major general in regular U. S. Army, 1812-14
> Won battle of New Orleans, 1815
> Member, U. S. Senate, 1823 (resigned, 1825)
> President of the United States, 1829-1837
> Died, 1845; buried at Hermitage beside wife
> Bronze statue unveiled at Capitol, 1928
> Statue located in Capitol Rotunda

Andrew Jackson was not gifted in letters... What he did have, however was a hard common sense; an almost unequaled natural ability; a wonderful physical and moral courage... perhaps unsurpassed in the history of this Republic; and he had a will to do that was invincible. These qualities are what made Andrew Jackson the great man that he was; and it was these qualities that made him live in history today and will always as long as the deeds of great men are revered... His kindly private life is a monument and inspiration to every one who believes in the purity and uprightness of the family life in America... His career as a citizen, as a statesman, as a builder in part of this great Republic, as a Congressman, as a Senator, a Judge, and as President was and will be an inspiration to men as long as time shall endure.— SENATOR KENNETH MCKELLAR of Tennessee. *From acceptance proceedings in the U. S. Senate*, April 16, 1928.

SAM HOUSTON

1793-1863

Sculptor, ELISABET NEY

STEPHEN F. AUSTIN

1793-1836

Sculptor, ELISABET NEY

Texas

SAM HOUSTON

He adopted Texas and Texas adopted him to her untold benefit

LIBERATOR, SOLDIER, STATESMAN
Born in Rockbridge County, Virginia, 1793
To Tennessee; lived near Cherokees, aged 12
In 7th U. S. Infantry at age of 20
In Creek War as 1st lieutenant, 1818
Studied law, Nashville; district att'y, 1819
Member, U. S. House of R., 1823-1827
Seventh governor of Tennessee, 1827
Resigned, 1829; lived among Cherokees
To Texas; led Texas forces against Mexico
First President, Texas Republic, 1836-1838
Took first step toward Texas annexation
Member, U. S. Senate, 1846-1859
Seventh governor of Texas, 1859-1861
Died in Huntsville, Texas, 1863
Marble statue accepted by Congress, 1905
Statue located in Statuary Hall

In a simple grave, devoid of show, lie the remains of the plain man and citizen who in life shunned all pretense and display. Around him, spread out in the golden glory of a southern sun, stretches out in boundless reaches of plain and prairie and plateau, the magnificent State he helped into being, protected in its infancy, and ably represented in these halls in its early maturity. The closing act of Houston's official life was in strict keeping with the character of the man. Being required to take the oath of allegiance to the new Confederacy into which Texas had entered, he could not cast lightly aside the fruits of that Union with the United States for which he had long and successfully labored. He declined to take the oath, resigned his position as Governor of Texas . . . carrying with him the high admiration, and the profound gratitude of all his fellow-citizens.—Hon. Samuel Bronson Cooper, M.C. of Texas. *From acceptance proceedings, February 25, 1905.*

STEPHEN F. AUSTIN

He was one colonizer in Texas who fulfilled his contract with Mexico

COLONIZER, PATRIOT
Born near Austinville, Virginia, 1793
Schools: New England; Ky.; Mo. frontier
Began colonizing Texas; father's wish, 1821
Mexico had colonizing contract with father
Traveled 1000 miles to Mexico City at once
Stephen got ratification of this contract
He then had judicial and military powers
Made first legal settlement, Texas, 1822
Violence disappeared under Stephen's rule
Wanted political justice under Mexican flag
To U. S. seeking Texas independence, 1835
He brought about Texas independence, 1836
First Secretary of State, Texas Republic
Died, 1836; gave his life to adopted state
Marble statue accepted by Congress, 1905
Statue located in Vestibule S. of Rotunda

With untiring zeal, with loftiest patriotism, with greatest conservative ability he labored to build up that territory (Texas) in the best interest of all the colonists who flocked not only to his standard but to the standards of many others who followed. His wise counsel was a tower of strength to the struggling colonists through all that stormy period which led to the establishment of the Texan Republic. Yoakum, who wrote one of the earliest and best histories of Texas, pays his memory this beautiful tribute, "If he who, by conquest, wins an empire and receives the world's applause, how much more is due to those who, by unceasing toil, lay in the wilderness the foundation for an infant colony, and build thereon a vigorous and happy State. Surely there is not among men a more honorable destiny than to be the peaceful founder and builder of a new Commonwealth. Such was the destiny of Stephen F. Austin."—Hon. George F. Burgess, M.C. of Texas. *From acceptance proceedings, February 25, 1905.*

ETHAN ALLEN

1737-1789

Sculptor, LARKIN G. MEAD

JACOB COLLAMER

1792-1865

Sculptor, PRESTON POWERS

Vermont

ETHAN ALLEN

He was the "Robin Hood" of the early New England frontier

REVOLUTIONARY SOLDIER, AUTHOR
Born in Litchfield, Conn., probably 1737
Little known of youth; father died, 1755
In iron business, Salisbury, Conn., 1762
Served in French and Indian War, 1757
Probably resident of Vermont by 1769
Colonel, Green Mountain Boys, 1770
Led opposition to N. Y. Claims for Vermont
Won fame, capture of Ft. Ticonderoga, 1775
Captured, held prisoner 2 years by British
Exchanged by Gen. Washington, 1778
Breveted colonel; maj. gen. Vt. Militia, 1779
Settled in Burlington, Vt., as farmer, 1787
Authored books, articles and addresses
Died of apoplexy at Burlington home, 1789
Marble statue accepted by Congress, 1876
Statue located in Statuary Hall

I have been happy in the exchange, and a visit from Lieutenant Colonel Ethan Allen. His fortitude and firmness seems to have placed him out of the reach of misfortune. There is an original something about him that commands admiration, and his long captivity and sufferings have only served to increase, if possible, his enthusiastic zeal. He appears very desirous of rendering his services to the states and of being employed, and at the same time he does not discover any ambition for high rank. Congress will herewith receive a letter from him, and I doubt not they will make such provision for him as they think proper and suitable. — GENERAL GEORGE WASHINGTON. *From a letter written to Congress from Valley Forge, May 12, 1778.*

The letter and Brevet for Colonel Allen I will transmit by the first opportunity. He left camp eight days ago. — GENERAL GEORGE WASHINGTON. *From a letter written to Congress from Valley Forge, May 18, 1778.*

JACOB COLLAMER

He gave a half century of varied and distinguished service to State and Nation

ORATOR, JURIST, STATESMAN
Born at Troy, New York, 1792
Family moved to Burlington, Vt., 1795
Country school; earned University expense
Graduate, University of Vermont, 1810
Served in militia on Canadian frontier, 1812
To Woodstock, Vt.; admitted to the bar, 1813
Member, Vt. Assembly, 1821-22; 1827-1828
Justice of the Vt. Supreme Court, 1833-1842
Delegate to Vt. Constitutional Conv., 1836
Member, U. S. House of R., 1843-1849
Postmaster General, by Pres. Taylor, 1949-50
Justice of the Vt. Supreme Court, 1850-1854
Member, U. S. Senate till death, 1855-1865
Died, Woodstock Vt. (brief illness), 1865
Marble statue accepted by Congress, 1881
Statue located in Hall of Columns

The distinguishd statesman, Jacob Collamer, whose statue is now presented under the act of Congress of 1864 by the state of Vermont, I knew well and intimately for several years. We entered Congress together in 1843 and remained in the House together until 1849 when he was appointed to the office of Postmaster General. During the three Congresses of our joint service we occupied adjacent seats. I well recollect Judge Collamer's first speech in the House. This speech, not over thirty minutes in length, was so pointed, clear, logical and conclusive that it put him at once in the front rank of debaters, lawyers, and jurists in the House . . . Jacob Collamer was a man of great probity, of most exemplary conduct, and of sincere piety, but never indulged in the expression of positive opinions or even speculations upon what he did not clearly understand in any sphere of thought. — HON. ALEXANDER H. STEPHENS, M.C. of Georgia. *From acceptance proceedings, 1881.*

ROBERT E. LEE

1807-1870

Sculptor, EDWARD V. VALENTINE

GEORGE WASHINGTON

1732-1799

Sculptor, EDWARD V. VALENTINE

Virginia

ROBERT E. LEE

He shares with Jefferson Davis the glory and tragedy of the "Lost Cause"

SOLDIER, CONFEDERATE LEADER
Born at "Stratford," Virginia, 1807
Son of "Light-Horse Harry Lee" of the Rev.
Moved with family to Alexandria, Va., 1811
Entered West Point, 1825; graduated, 1829
Married Mary Ann Custis at Arlington, 1831
At Washington with Chief Engineer, 1834-37
Captain of Engineers, 1838; colonel, 1848
Officer under Gen. Scott, Mexican War, 1847
Supt. West Point, 1852; Arlington, 1857
Left U. S. Army, 1861; went with Virginia
Distinguished Confederatee general, 1861-65
Surrendered, Gen. Grant, Appomattox, 1865
President, Washington Coll., Lexington, Va.
Died at Lexington, Virginia, 1870
Bronze statue placed in Capitol, 1908
Statue located in Statuary Hall

In presenting the measures providing that the statue of Lee should accompany that of Washington in our National Valhalla, I do so from no desire to offend Northern sentiment . . . but rather from entirely opposite motives. I believed then . . . that such a gesture by Virginia would be as it was intended to be, of great moment toward strengthening the ties that now bind together the once divided North and South into one great reunited country in which sectionalism is dead and buried.—JUDGE DON P. HALSEY of Virginia. *From acceptance program*, May 18, 1934.

The animosities engendered by the Civil War have long since been obliterated. The Mason and Dixon line is no longer even a figure of speech. As time marches on the pioneer states which share a common ancestry and similar histories tend more than ever to a common consciousness and community of interest and spirit.—SENATOR DAVID I. WALSH, Massachusetts. *From acceptance program*, May 18, 1934.

GEORGE WASHINGTON

"First in war, first in peace, and first in the hearts of his countrymen"

"FATHER OF HIS COUNTRY"
Born at "Wakefield," in Virginia, 1732
Parish sexton, early teacher; tutor, 1743
At Mt. Vernon with brother Lawrence, 1749
Inherited Mt. Vernon from Lawrence, 1752
Colonel, French and Indian Wars, 1754-58
Va. legislator, 1758-74; married, 1759
In 1st & 2nd Continental Congresses, 1774-75
Commander, Revolutionary War, 1775-83
Resigned from Army, 1783; to Mt. Vernon
President, Constitutional Convention, 1787
President of The United States, 1789-1797
Farewell Address, 1796; retirement, 1797-99
Called from retirement; National crisis, 1798
Died, Mt. Vernon, 1799; buried, Mt. Vernon
Bronze statue placed in Capitol, 1908
Statue located in Capitol Rotunda

Mr. President, though I am truly sensible of the high honor done me, in this appointment, yet I feel great distress from a consciousness that my ability and military experience may not be equal to the extensive and important trust: However, as the Congress desire it, I will enter upon the momentous duty, and exert every power I possess in their service, and for support of the glorious cause . . . As to pay, Sir, I beg leave to assure the Congress that, as no pecuniary consideration could have tempted me to have accepted this arduous employment, at the expense of my domestic ease and happiness, I do not wish to make any profit from it. I will keep an exact account of my expenses, and that is all I desire.—COLONEL GEORGE WASHINGTON. *From Journals of the Continental Congress*, 1775.

To add brightness to the sun, or glory to the name of Washington is alike impossible. Let none attempt it. In solemn awe we pronounce the name, and in its naked, deathless splendor leave it shining on.—ABRAHAM LINCOLN.

FRANCIS H. PIERPONT

1814-1899

Sculptor, FRANKLIN SIMMONS

JOHN E. KENNA

1848-1893

Sculptor, ALEXANDER DOYLE

West Virginia

FRANCIS H. PIERPONT

His loyalty to the Union appropriately caused his fathering of West Virginia

"FATHER OF WEST VIRGINIA"
Born in Monongalia Co., now West Va., 1814
Graduate, Meadville, Pa. College, 1839
Became teacher, lawyer, businessman
Always an active Christian worker
Provisional Governor, Virginia, 1861
Seat of government to Richmond, 1865
Served Virginia as Governor, 1862-1868
To home in Fairmont, West Virginia, 1868
Elected, House of Delegates, West Va., 1869
Collector, internal revenue, West Va.
Appointed to this office by Pres. Garfield
Pierpont was never governor of West Va.
Died at Fairmont, West Virginia, 1899
Buried, Woodlawn Cemetery, near Fairmont
Marble statue unveiled at Capitol, 1910
Statue located in Statuary Hall

Governor Pierpont was the conservative leader who made it possible by legal methods to constitute the State of West Virginia. He was conservative . . . but when his duty was made plain then he became the aggressive, earnest, capable leader, brave and daring, fearing only not to do right. No more patriotic citizen ever lived in the Commonwealth over whose affairs he had control for nearly 8 years. I refer of course to the State of Virginia. . . . He loyally supported President Lincoln throughout the civil conflict and rendered efficient aid toward the suppression of the rebellion. . . . In beautiful Woodlawn Cemetery near the town which was his home for nearly three quarters of a century, lie the remains of the noble character whose pure life and whose lofty patriotism we commemorate at this hour. On his tomb is chiseled the phrase, "Father of West Virginia," and just below, with even a higher meaning and loftier strain we read, "Patriot, Statesman, Christian."—Hon. Thomas C. Miller. *From unveiling ceremony*, April 30, 1910.

JOHN E. KENNA

Died at 45, having served his state 16 years in Congress as Representative and Senator

SOLDIER, STATESMAN
Born Kanawha Co., Va., now W. Va., 1848
Family left poor when father died in 1856
With mother went to live with uncle in Mo.
Pioneer conditions; little early schooling
Young Kenna joined Confederate Army, 1864
Wounded in action; to West Virginia, 1865
At. St. Vincents College, Wheeling, 3 years
Admitted to bar, Charleston, W. Va., 1870
Prosecuting Attorney, Kanawha Co., 1872-77
Circuit Court Justice, home district, 1875
Member, U. S. House of R., 1877-1883
Member, U. S. Senate, 1883-1893 (till death)
Died in D. C., 1893; services in U. S. Senate
Buried in Charleston, West Virginia
Marble statue placed in Capitol, 1901
Statue located in Hall of Columns

In the face of mighty sorrow the tongue refuses to speak all that wells up in the heart for utterance. . . . Measured by years, John E. Kenna was one of the youngest Members in this Chamber, not yet 45 years of age; but measured by the accomplishments of his life, he ranked with the octogenarian. Whether as soldier or as citizen, as husband, father, or friend, he had rounded out a life and leaves behind him a record to challenge the approval of mankind. Measured as a lawyer or lawmaker, he left his impress upon the generation to which he belonged. He has engraven in ineffaceable characters upon the history of his country his achievements here and in the other branch of the National Legislature. Kindly as a woman, unselfish to a fault, brave and unflinching in the discharge of every duty, it has never been my good fortune to come in contact with a nature more lovable or more exalted, than that of our dead comrade. — Senator J. C. S. Blackburn, Kentucky. *From The Congressional Record*, January 11, 1893.

ROBERT MARION LAFOLLETTE

1855-1925

Sculptor, JO DAVIDSON

JAMES MARQUETTE

1637-1675

Sculptor, C. TRENTANOVE

Wisconsin

ROBERT MARION LaFOLLETTE

He was a modern knight in armor fighting valiantly for his people

> SAGE, PROPHET, STATESMAN
> Born in Primrose, Dane Co., Wisconsin, 1855
> Early learned not to despise labor
> And early training taught him self-reliance
> Graduate, U. of Wisconsin, Madison, 1879
> Admitted to bar the following year
> Began law practice at Madison, Wisc., 1880
> District Attorney, Dane County, 1880-84
> Member, U. S. House of R., 1885-1891
> Resumed practice of law in Madison
> Wisconsin Governor, 1901-1906 (resigned)
> Member, U. S. Senate, 1906 till death
> Lost race for Presidency, 1924
> Died in Washington, D. C., 1925
> Buried in Madison, Wisconsin
> Marble statue unveiled at Capitol, 1929
> Statue located in Statuary Hall

Father first took me through Statuary Hall. He knew that critics found fault with some statues as works of art. But his intimate knowledge of history made him venerate not the statues but the lives they commemorated. Washngton, Jackson, Lincoln, Jefferson and the others were not just names. Each stood for a definite, vital force in the creation of a nation and the preservation of its ideal of human liberty and democracy.— PHILIP F. LAFOLLETTE. *Unveiling,* April 25, 1929.

Robert LaFollette felt the pulse beat of the heart of humanity.... He devoted his life to public service, not for his own advancement but in the spirit he well expressed in *The Making of America:* "It is a glorious service —this service for the country. Each one should count it a patriotic duty to build at least a part of his life into the life of his country, to do his share in the making of America according to the plan of the fathers!" —SENATOR JOHN J. BLAINE, Wisconsin. *From unveiling ceremony,* April 25, 1929.

JAMES MARQUETTE

He braved the untrodden wilderness and risked all for God and King

> EXPLORER, JESUIT MISSIONARY
> Born, France, 1637; in Jesuit College, 1654
> Missionary, New France, America, 1666
> Studied Indian languages 2 years at Quebec
> With Ottawa Indians, 1668; St. Ignace, 1671
> Held it his duty to contribute to knowledge
> Began search for "south-running river," 1673
> With Joliet journeyed 3000 miles in canoes
> Found waterway to Gulf of Mexico
> After Mississippi trip, rested at Mackinac
> Headed for new Mission in present Ill., 1674
> Became ill; died on trip to Mackinac, 1675
> Indians removed body to St. Ignace, 1676
> Marquette kept journal of famous voyage
> *Marquette's Journal* was published, 1681
> Marble statue accepted by Senate, 1896
> Statue located in House Connection

Separated as were Marquette and LaFollette by more than two centuries in time, and engaged in radically different lines of work, the lives of these two citizens of Wisconsin yet present many parallels, and both typify the ideals and aspirations of the people of Wisconsin. Both men were of unsullied character, beloved by all who knew them. Both were inspired by the love of their fellow men. Both possessed undaunted courage. Both were pioneers in the truest sense of the word —the one in the field of exploration, the other in the field of government.... Marquette voluntarily left a place of scholarly seclusion in France to carry the message of the lowly Nazarene to the savage Indians in the heart of the wilderness and lost his life in this enterprise. He saw the squalor and savagery of the Indian and gave his life in the effort to alleviate his lowly brother.—SENATOR JOHN J. BLAINE, Wisconsin. *From unveiling ceremony,* April 25, 1929.

One Statue Each

ARIZONA
John Campbell Greenway

LOUISIANA
Huey Pierce Long

MINNESOTA
Henry Mower Rice

SOUTH DAKOTA
William Henry Harrison Beadle

UTAH
Brigham Young

WASHINGTON
Marcus Whitman

JOHN CAMPBELL GREENWAY

1872-1926

Sculptor, GUTZON BORGLUM

HUEY PIERCE LONG

1893-1935

Sculptor, CHARLES KECK

Arizona

JOHN CAMPBELL GREENWAY

Not as an office holder but as an engineer he helped to build the West

> SOLDIER, INDUSTRIALIST
> Born in Huntsville, Alabama, 1872
> Attended University of Virginia and Phillips Academy, Andover, Mass.
> Graduate of Yale University, 1895
> Foreman, Carnegie Steel Co., Duquesne, Pa.
> Asst. Mine Supt. in Michigan, 1899-1906
> Mgr. Calumet & Arizona Mining Co., 1910
> Mgr. New Cornelia Mining Company
> Built the mining town of Ajo, Arizona
> Served in France, First World War
> Distinguished at Chateau-Thierry; St. Mihiel
> Col. of Infantry, 1919; Brig. general, 1922
> Resumed business activity at war's close
> Died in 1926; buried on Ajo estate
> Bronze statue unveiled at Capitol, 1930
> Statue located in Statuary Hall

There was superb romance in the career of General Greenway; he was laborer, captain of industry, athlete, soldier, idealist, philosopher, and philanthropist; moreover, he had many other title deeds to our grateful remembrance—attributes which were stronger than wealth, office or power could bestow, for he was a man of inflexible integrity and unsullied character. There was about his personality a majestic Roman dignity and a true and pure modesty. His eyes flashed far into the future and carried a message of good faith. In all enterprises for the upbuilding and the progress of our common Country he participated with the enthusiasm of the pioneer and the charm of the poet, for he was a man of great energy and real creative genius. He adored the flag of his Country; he had a firm devotion to American institutions, and his unbreakable belief in the power of truth and courage was the diamond pivot upon which his daily life revolved.—SENATOR HENRY F. ASHURST, Arizona. *From the unveiling ceremony*, May 24, 1930.

Louisiana

HUEY PIERCE LONG

He illustrates the possible storms of political life even in Democratic America

> PHILOSOPHER, STATESMAN
> Born near Winnfield, Louisiana, 1893
> Worked part time as printer at age of 13
> But was forced to leave High School at 17
> Early earned his living as a salesman
> Attended Oklahoma University at Norman
> Admitted to bar at Winnfield, La., 1915
> Railroad Commissioner, Shreveport, 1918-28
> Lost governorship nomination, 1924
> Governor of Louisiana, 1928-1932
> Elected to the United States Senate, 1931
> Served as U. S. Senator from La. till death
> Died at Baton Rouge, Louisiana, 1935
> Death result of gunshot wound by assassin
> Buried in Capitol Grounds at Baton Rouge
> Bronze statue unveiled in Capitol, 1941
> Statue located in Statuary Hall

Huey Long was always a student. He had a profound knowledge of the Holy Bible. He never finished his education. Until the night when he was felled by an assassin's bullet he was a pupil, a learner, an inquirer, a seeker of knowledge. He was a great lawyer. He always endeavored to get at the truth, at the very core of a case. He had a clear head and a good heart. He fought for the poor and oppressed with his convincing oratory, with his pen, with his wits, with his great intellect and knowledge of human character. . . . Huey Long was not a dictator. He was a doer of things for the benefit of the masses; and his philosophy of distribution of wealth, his advocacy of pensions for the aged, shorter working hours for labor and his continued fight for the masses, which marked him for death, will remain as a challenge to true democracy in this treasured land of ours.—SENATOR ALLEN J. ELLENDER, Louisiana. *From acceptance proceedings in the U. S. Senate*, April 25, 1941.

HENRY MOWER RICE

1817-1894

Sculptor, F. E. TRIEBEL

WILLIAM HENRY HARRISON BEADLE

1838-1915

Sculptor, H. Daniel Webster

Minnesota

HENRY MOWER RICE

He was influential in etsablishing basic foundations for the Commonwealth of Minnesota

> STATE BUILDER, STATESMAN
> Born in Waitsfield, Vermont, 1817
> Held a surveyor's job, Detroit, Mich.
> To Ft. Snelling, Minn., for U. S. Army, 1839
> Made treaties with Chippewas, 1847
> Adjusted differences with the Sioux, 1852
> Lobbied in Washington for a Minn. Territory
> Delegate for Minn. Territory, 1853-1857
> Instrumental in Minnesota statehood
> Member, U. S. Senate, from Minn., 1858-63
> Chippewas called him "White Rice"
> President, State Historical Society
> Member, Board of Regents, U. of Minnesota
> Treasurer, Ramsey County, 1878-1884
> Died in Texas, 1894; buried, St. Paul, Minn.
> Marble statue unveiled at Capitol, 1916
> Statue located in Statuary Hall

Henry M. Rice will loom up over the vista of the passing years as one of the great men who cradled and nursed our State in its infancy and breathed into it the spirit and life that matured it into a great Commonwealth. The progress and welfare of the Territory and young State were near to his heart, and his zeal and activity never slackened in its behalf. He was emphatically a great state builder, whose vision and the effect of whose work extended into the distant future. We of the present generation have reaped, most bountifully reaped, where he, under many drawbacks and difficulties, sowed.... He was handsome, genial and kind hearted, always ready to help and serve.... He was an orator of action, not words. His love for his adopted State and for the Federal Union was paramount, pure and untarnished. In the hour of the Nation's great distress he never faltered in words or deeds.—SENATOR KNUTE NELSON, Minnesota. *From unveiling ceremony, February 8, 1916.*

South Dakota

WILLIAM HENRY HARRISON BEADLE

He merits honor for the "Gift Magnificent" to education—public school lands

> SOLDIER, EDUCATOR
> Born in Parke County, Indiana, 1838
> Early education in country school
> Used $1000 gift for a college education
> Entered U. of Mich. 1857; graduated, 1861
> Had five years' service in the Civil War
> Discharged a brigadier general, 1866
> Obtained a law degree at the U. of Mich.
> Surveyor General, Dakota Territory, 1869
> Territory Supt. of Public Instruction, 1879
> Held school lands for maximum benefits
> Promoted township school organization
> President, Madison Normal School, 1889-1906
> History Prof. Madison Normal Sch., 1906-12
> Died at home of daughter in Calif., 1915
> Bronze statue unveiled in Capitol, 1938
> Statue located in Statuary Hall

William Beadle has earned the title of America's first conservationist. As a crusader he won the hearts of the Dakotans, and ultimately saved twenty million acres of school lands in South Dakota, North Dakota, Montana, Washington, Idaho and Wyoming. He was apparently the first individual to realize the value of endowment lands to a developing society. Under the old system, school lands had been used to create immediate values in the neighborhoods where they lay. Beadle proposed to let the social development affect the school lands, thereby enhancing their value for the future and permanent benefit of the schools. His tenacity carried him through a twenty-year struggle to protect the permanent school funds by provisions in the newly created state constitutions and bylaws which were enacted in other states. He insisted upon a permanent school fund, the principle forever to remain inviolate with only the earnings to be used for school support.—SENATOR HERBERT E. HITCHCOCK of South Dakota. *NEA Broadcast*, Feb. 23, 1938.

BRIGHAM YOUNG

1801-1877

Sculptor, MAHONRI MACKINTOSH YOUNG

MARCUS WHITMAN

1802-1847

Sculptor, AVARD FAIRBANKS

Utah

BRIGHAM YOUNG

With faith like Moses he led his people to the "Promised Land"

> PIONEER, EMPIRE BUILDER
> Born in Whitingham, Vermont, 1801
> The Young family were devout Puritans
> Father taught him Bible; mother, reading
> Mother died, 1815; apprenticed same year
> Set up business as cabinet maker, 1817
> Home in N. Y. Heard of "Book of Mormon"
> Visited Joseph Smith; joined church, 1832
> Church leader at death of Prophet Smith
> Brigham Young then led his people West
> They were seeking religious freedom
> Trusted guide in spiritual and economic life
> Conquered desert; founded western Empire
> From Commonwealth came State of Utah
> Died in Salt Lake City, Utah, 1877
> Marble statue unveiled at Capitol, 1950
> Statue located in Statuary Hall

These great pioneers of ours who carried democracy, who carried the freedom of worship, the freedom of speech, the freedom of the press, and the freedom of assembly out into these vast lands in the West and Middle West were building a civilization, building a way of life, building the very bedrock and foundation of all that we cherish today and all for which we are willing to fight as inheritors of the great heritage handed down to us from the past which makes us proud, not simply of our ancestry politically or religiously or otherwise but makes us proud of the institutions which they built up and which it is our mission, as I see it, for us to preserve at all hazards and at all costs. We have become the leaders among the Nations of the world. . . . Fate and Destiny have put into our hands the torch of leadership. — ALBEN W. BARKLEY, Vice President of the United States. *From unveiling ceremony, June 1, 1950.*

Washington

MARCUS WHITMAN

He was the first Christian Missionary to Oregon, our Pacific Northwest

> MISSIONARY, COLONIZER, DOCTOR
> Born in Rushville, New York, 1802
> Father, shoemaker and tanner, died, 1809
> At 17 Marcus active church worker
> Began the study of medicine in Rushville
> "Rode out" with experienced doctor, 2 years
> Diploma, Fairfield medical school, 1826
> Country practice, horseback, upper N. Y.
> Longed to be a western medical missionary
> Made an exploratory trip West in 1835
> He and wife to Oregon Territory, 1836
> Made first American home on Pacific coast
> Sought help in East for Oregon Terr., 1842
> Brought wagon train West to Oregon, 1843
> He and wife massacred by Indians, 1847
> Bronze statue unveiled at Capitol, 1953
> Statue located in Statuary Hall

The establishment of the Whitmans' Mission and their labors with white and red men alike called for vision, courage, hardship, and sacrifice. They died at their post of duty like soldiers in battle, but they did not die in vain, for memory lives in the pages of history, and in the hearts of every loyal American citizen and lover of courage. — WALTER MEACHAM, Old Oregon Trail, Inc.

There has been no other couple like the Whitmans in American history — no wooing more strange, no wedding more extraordinary, no marriage more proof against stress and storm, no union of purpose and effort more perfect, no failure more pathetic, no ending more terrible, and no immortality more sublime than theirs. So greatly did they live, so magnificently did they labor and serve, that forces they set in motion will forever enrich the civilization they helped to plant on the western slopes of the Continental Divide. — DR. CHESTER MAXEY, Pres., Whitman College. *Unveiling,* May 22, 1953.

Statues Not Given by States

EDWARD DICKINSON BAKER
Purchased by Congress, 1873

BENJAMIN FRANKLIN
By commission, 1863

GENERAL ULYSSES S. GRANT
Presented by G.A.R., 1900

ALEXANDER HAMILTON
By commission, 1868

JOHN HANCOCK
By commission, 1861

THOMAS JEFFERSON
Ordered by commission, 1855

THOMAS JEFFERSON
Gift of Capt. Uriah P. Levy, 1834

ABRAHAM LINCOLN
By commission, 1871

EDWARD DICKINSON BAKER

1811-1861

Sculptor, HORATIO STONE

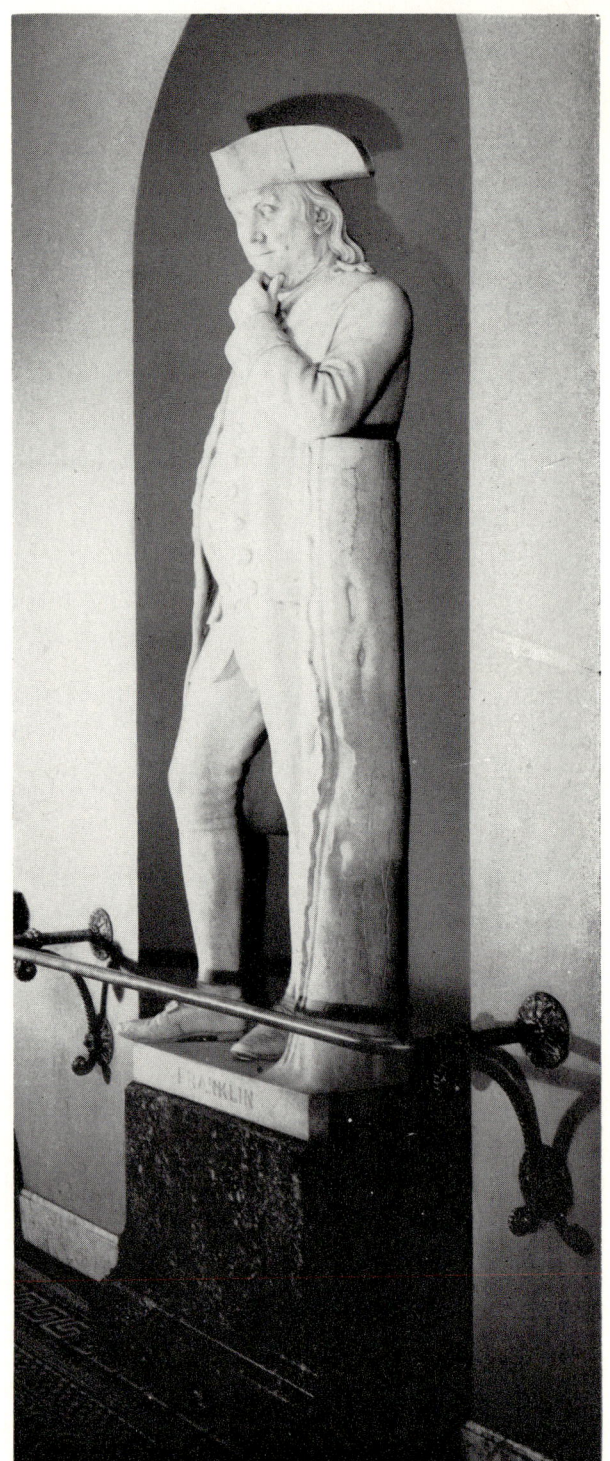

BENJAMIN FRANKLIN

1706-1790

Sculptor, HIRAM POWERS

EDWARD DICKINSON BAKER

He was dedicated to Freedom's cause in legislative halls or on fields of battle

SOLDIER, STATESMAN
Born in London, England, 1811
To Philadelphia, 1815; to Illinois, 1825
Began law practice, Springfield, Ill., 1830
In Ill. House of R., 1837; Ill. Senate, 1840
In U. S. House of R., 1845-46 (resigned)
Colonel, Volunteer Infantry, 1846
Member, U. S. House of R., 1849-1851
To San Francisco law practice, 1851
Moved to State of Oregon in 1860
In U. S. Senate from Ore., Oct. 2, 1860
Brig. general and major general in 1861
Killed at Balls Bluff, Va., Oct. 21, 1861
Buried in San Francisco National Cemetery
Marble statue erected in Capitol, 1873
Statue purchased by act of Congress
Statue located in Capitol Rotunda

Mr. Speaker, Colonel Baker fulfilled the prophetic words which he uttered on this floor in 1850. He said, at the conclusion of one of his speeches, "I have only to say that if the time should come when disunion rules the hour and discord is to reign supreme, I shall again be ready to give the best blood in my veins in my country's cause. I shall be prepared to do battle in every land in defense of the Constitution of the country which I have sworn to support." He has fulfilled the prophecy.—HON. WILLIAM A. RICHARDSON, M.C. of Illinois. *From The Congressional Globe,* January 22, 1862.

His faults, which were few, were those of the generous and social; his virtues were many and heroic. Deeply ingrained in his nature was a love of freedom; a reverence for free institutions, free men and a pleasure in the elevation of the masses that no demagogue can appreciate.—HON. AARON A. SARGENT, M.C. of Calif. *From The Congressional Globe,* January 22, 1862.

BENJAMIN FRANKLIN

An outstanding "Founding Father," with Adams, Hamilton, Jefferson, Washington

SIGNER, DECL. OF INDEPENDENCE
Born, Boston, 1706; little formal education
Had early tutor; learned art of printing
Worked in Boston, Philadelphia, London
Established printing business in Phila.
Owned Pa. Gazette, 1728; Almanac, 1732
Clerk, Pa. Gen. Assembly, 1736-50; P.M., 1737
Member, Provincial Assembly, 1744-1754
Elected member, scientific "Royal Society"
Agent, Pa. to London, 1757-62, 1764-75
Member, Continental Congress, 1775, 1776
Pres. Pa. Constitutional Convention, 1776
Minister, France, 1776-85; Gov. of Pa., 1785
Signer, Dec'l of Ind. and the Constitution
Died, Phila., 1790; Christ Church burial
Marble statue received in Capitol, 1863
Executed by commission; in Senate Annex

Mr. Speaker, as we have been informed not only through the channel of the newspapers, but by a more direct communication, of the decease of an illustrious character, whose native genius has rendered distinguished services to the cause of mankind in general; and whose patriotic exertions have contributed in a high degree to the independence and prosperity of this country in particular, the occasion seems to call upon us to pay some tribute to his memory expressive of the tender veneration his country feels for such distinguished merit. I, therefore, move the following resolution: "The House being informed of the decease of Benjamin Franklin, a citizen whose native genius was not more an ornament to human nature, than his various exertions of it have been precious to science, to freedom, and to his country, do resolve, as a mark of the veneration due to his memory, that the Members wear the customary badge of mourning for one month. — JAMES MADISON, M.C. of Virginia. *From the Congressional Globe,* April 22, 1790.

GENERAL ULYSSES S. GRANT

1822-1885

Sculptor, FRANKLIN SIMMONS

ALEXANDER HAMILTON

1757-1804

Sculptor, HORATIO STONE

GENERAL ULYSSES S. GRANT

Competent commander of greatest military force in modern history up to his time

PRESIDENT OF THE UNITED STATES
Born in Clermont County, Ohio, 1822
Entered Military Academy, West Point, 1839
Graduate, West Point, 1843; in Mexican War
Resigned from Army, 1859; to Illinois, 1860
Col., Ill. Volunteers, 1861; maj. gen., 1862
Maj. gen., U. S. Army, 1863; Lt. Gen., 1864
Great American Civil War general
Congress created "General of the Armies"
General Grant appointed to this rank, 1866
President of the United States, 1869-1877
Retired by Congress; rank of General, 1885
Died at Mt. McGregor, N. Y., 1885
Buried at Riverside Park, New York City
Marble statue accepted by Congress, 1900
Statue located in Capitol Rotunda
Gift of The Grand Army of the Republic

This statue of General Grant is a tribute of the affectionate regard of his old companions in arms. They take honest pride in his fame, which is in part their own. . . . We feel that his fame is the common heritage of the Nation, and that in it we can all take pride. It is a very remarkable thing, and one highly creditable to all concerned, that there should be such unanimity of feeling toward the chief military leader of a great and recent Civil War. But strange as it may seem to people of other countries, the name of General Grant is loved and honored, North and South. The North remembers and honors him for his unfaltering courage in the hour of danger: the South remembers and loves him for his unvarying kindness in the hour of triumph. All of his countrymen, North and South, unite in admiration for his genius and affection for his character. — HON. JAMES THOMPSON MCCLEARY, M.C. of Minnesota. *From acceptance proceedings,* May 19, 1900.

ALEXANDER HAMILTON

"He smote the rock of federal finance and abundant streams of revenue gushed forth"

SOLDIER, STATESMAN, FINANCIER
Born in British West Indies, 1757
Immigrated to the United States, 1772
Attended King's College, now Columbia U.
Entered Continental Army in N. Y., 1776
Aide-de-camp to Gen. Washington, 1777-1781
In Continental Congress, 1782-83; 1787-88
Member, N. Y. State Assembly, 1787
Member, Constitutional Convention, 1787
Member, N. Y. State Convention, 1788
Admitted to the bar in New York City
First Secretary of the Treasury, 1789-1795
Returned to New York and practice of law
Mortally wounded in a duel with Burr, 1804
Died, 1804; buried in Trinity Churchyard
Marble statue erected in Capitol, 1868
Procured by commission; located in Rotunda

Here stands the Memorial to a great lover of liberty, a great patriot, a great soldier, a colossal statesman, a mighty American. Time has brought our appraisal of him out of the mists of misunderstanding and given us a measure of his true greatness. If I were to select one attribute above all others for the inspiration of Americans of today and the morrow, it would not be his brilliance of mind, or his gift of eloquence, or his matchless genius, or his prophetic vision; but I should commend his courage of patriotism, which put his devotion to the Republic's welfare before popular approval or personal fortune, and his unconditional gift of heart, mind and soul to the making of an imperishable temple of freedom in these United States. — WARREN G. HARDING, President of the United States. *From an address at the erection of the Hamilton Memorial at the Treasury Building,* Washington, D. C., May 17, 1923.

JOHN HANCOCK

1737-1793

Sculptor, HORATIO STONE

THOMAS JEFFERSON

1743-1826

Sculptor, HIRAM POWERS

JOHN HANCOCK

He dared to speak and act courageously against tyranny of George III

> SIGNER, DECL. OF INDEPENDENCE
> Born in Quincy, Massachusetts, 1737
> Graduated from Harvard College, 1754
> President, Boston Provincial Congress, 1774
> Active in pre-Revolutionary movements
> In Continental Congress, 1775-80, 1785, 1786
> Pres. Continental Congress, 1775 (2½ yrs.)
> First signer, Declaration of Independence
> Major general in Revolutionary War
> In Mass. Constitutional Convention, 1780
> Governor of Massachusetts, 1780-1785
> President, Continental Congress, 1785-1786
> (Resigned without serving because of illness)
> Governor of Massachusetts, 1787-1793
> Died, Quincy, Mass., 1793; buried in Boston
> Marble statue erected in Capitol, 1861
> Procured by commission; in Senate Annex

Resolved, that the proceedings of the American Continental Congress . . . reported by the honorable Delegates from this Colony, have with the deliberation due to their high importance been considered by us; and the American Bill of Rights therein contained appears to be formed with the greatest ability and judgment; to be founded on the immutable laws of nature and reason, the principles of the English constitution, and respective charters and constitutions of the colonies, and to be worthy of their most vigorous support, as essentially necessary to liberty. . . . Acknowledgments are due to the truly honorable and patriotic Members of the Continental Congress (John Hancock and others) for their wise and able exertions in the cause of American Liberty; and this Congress, in their own names and in behalf of this Colony, do hereby, with the utmost Sincerity, express the same . . . — CREDENTIALS OF DELEGATES. *From Massachusetts Bay Colony to the 2nd Continental Congress. From Journals of the Continental Congress,* December 5, 1774.

THOMAS JEFFERSON

Peerless founder and leader of America's Democratic Party

> PRESIDENT OF THE UNITED STATES
> Born in Old Shadwell, Virginia, 1743
> Graduate of William and Mary College, 1762
> Admitted to the bar, began practice, 1767
> Member, Colonial Legislature, 1769-1774
> Member, Continental Congress, 1775-1776
> Signed Decl. of Independence, Aug. 2, 1776
> Governor of Virginia, 1779-1781
> Member, Continental Congress, 1783-1785
> Minister to France (by Congress), 1784-1788
> Sec'y of State (by Pres. Washington), 1789-93
> Vice Pres. of The United States, 1797-1801
> President of The United States, 1801-1809
> Retired to estate, "Monticello," Va., 1809
> Died, Monticello, July 4, 1826; buried there
> Marble statue order, 1855; in Capitol, 1863
> Procured by commission; in House Annex

Today in the midst of a great war for freedom, we dedicate a shrine to freedom. To Thomas Jefferson, apostle of freedom, we are paying a debt long overdue. Yet there are reasons for gratitude that this occasion falls within our time; for our generation of Americans can understand much in Jefferson's life which intervening generations could not see as well as we. He faced the fact that men who will not fight for liberty can lose it. We, too, have faced that fact. He lived in a world in which freedom of conscience and freedom of mind were battles still to be fought through —not principles already accepted of all men. We, too, have lived in such a world. He loved peace and loved liberty—yet on more than one occasion he was forced to choose between them. We, too, have been compelled to make that choice.—FRANKLIN D. ROOSEVELT, President of The United States. *At the dedication of the Thomas Jefferson Memorial, Washington, D. C., April 13, 1943.*

THOMAS JEFFERSON

1743-1826

Sculptor, DAVID D'ANGERS

ABRAHAM LINCOLN

1809-1865

Sculptor, VINNIE REAM

THOMAS JEFFERSON

He was zealous of human freedom, physical, intellectual, spiritual

> AUTHOR, DECL. OF INDEPENDENCE
> Prominent in revolutionary writings
> *A Summary View*, delegate instruction, 1774
> *Declaration on Taking Arms*, July 6, 1775
> *Declaration of Independence*, July 4, 1776
> *Act for Religious Freedom*, in Virginia, 1779
> *Jefferson's Manual*, parliamentary procedure
> *Notes on Virginia*, printed in Paris, 1782
> *Philosophy of Jesus*, assembled, 1809
> Founded Univ. of Virginia; charter, 1819
> Voluminous correspondent with world leaders
> 18,000 Jefferson letters available today
> Last letter to Capital City, June 24, 1826
> Bronze statue first in Capitol Rotunda, 1834
> Statue on White House Grounds, 1835-1874
> Statue again placed in Capitol Rotunda, 1874
> Statue, gift of Captain Uriah P. Leavy

. . . May it (The Declaration of Independence) be to the world what I believe it will be, to some parts sooner, to others later, but finally to all, the signal of arousing men to burst the chains under which monkish ignorance and superstition had persuaded them to bind themselves, and to assume the blessings and security of self-government. . . All eyes are opened, or opening, to the rights of man. The general spread of the light of science has already laid open to every view the palpable truth, that the mass of mankind has not been born with saddles on their backs, nor a favored few, booted and spurred, ready to ride them legitimately, by the grace of God. These are grounds of hope for others. For ourselves, let the annual return of this day forever refresh our recollections of these rights, and an undiminished devotion to them. . .—THOMAS JEFFERSON. *From Jefferson's last letter*, written ten days before death, declining invitation to the Capital celebration, July 4, 1826

ABRAHAM LINCOLN

He saved the Union and abolished chattel slavery in the United States

> PRESIDENT OF THE UNITED STATES
> Born in Hardin County, Kentucky, 1809
> Parents to Indiana, 1816; log-cabin school
> With father moved to Illinois, 1830
> Read law and books on surveying
> Fought in Black Hawk War, 1832
> Postmaster, New Salem, Illinois, 1833
> In Ill. House of R., 1834, 1836, 1838, 1840
> Admitted to bar, 1836; to Springfield, 1837
> Member, U. S. House of R., 1847-1849
> Candidate, U. S. Senate, 1855 (lost)
> Candiate, U. S. Senate, 1858 (lost)
> President of the United States, 1861-65
> Shot, Ford's Theater, D. C., April 14, 1865
> Died, April 15; buried, Springfield, Ill.
> Marble statue unveiled at Capitol, 1871
> Procured by commission; located in Rotunda

Justice, truth, patience, mercy and love of his kind; simplicity, courage, sacrifice and confidence in God were his moral qualities. Clarity of thought and intellectual honesty, self-analysis and strong inexorable logic, supreme common sense, a sympathetic but unerring knowledge of human nature, imagination and limpid purity of style, with a poetic rhythm of the Psalms—these were his intellectual and cultural traits.—WILLIAM HOWARD TAFT, ex-President. *At dedication of Lincoln Memorial on the banks of the Potomac, in Washington, D. C.*, May 30, 1922.

The most important object is the statue of Lincoln, which is placed in the center of the Memorial, and by virtue of its imposing position in the place of honor, the gentleness, power and intelligence of the man, expressed as far as possible by the sculptor's art, predominate. This portion of the Memorial where the statue is placed is unoccupied by any other object that might detract from it.—HENRY BACON, Architect, Lincoln Memorial.

National Statuary Hall Epitomizes the Story of America

I. BEGINNING A GREAT NARRATIVE
1607-1770

John Winthrop, *Massachusetts, 1588-1649*
Junipero Serra, *California, 1713-1784*
James Marquette, *Wisconsin, 1637-1675*
Roger Williams, *Rhode Island, 1604-1683*
John Stark, *New Hampshire, 1728-1822*
George Washington, *Virginia, 1732-1799*

II. STORY OF AMERICAN INDEPENDENCE
1770-1800

1. DECLARING INDEPENDENCE

Samuel Adams, *Massachusetts, 1722-1803*
John Hancock, *1737-1793**
Roger Sherman, *Connecticut, 1721-1793*
Thomas Jefferson, *1743-1826**
Benjamin Franklin, *1706-1790**
Richard Stockton, *New Jersey, 1730-1781*
Charles Carroll, *Maryland, 1737-1832*
Caesar Rodney, *Delaware, 1728-1784*

2. FIGHTING FOR IDEPENDENCE

George Washington, *Virginia, 1732-1799*
Nathaniel Greene, *Rhode Island, 1742-1786*
Alexander Hamilton, *1757-1804**
Caesar Rodney, *Delaware, 1728-1784*
Jonathan Trumbull, *Connecticut, 1710-1785*
George Clinton, *New York, 1739-1812*
Ethan Allen, *Vermont, 1737-1789*
J. P. G. Muhlenberg, *Pennsylvania, 1746-1807*

3. FOUNDATIONS FOR LOCAL SELF-GOVERNMET

Jonathan Trumbull, *Connecticut, 1710-1785*
Samuel Adams, *Massachusetts, 1722-1803*
George Clinton, *New York, 1739-1812*
John Hancock, *1737-1793**
John Hanson, *Maryland, 1715-1783*
Robert R. Livingston, *New York, 1746-1813*

4. FOUNDATIONS FOR NATIONAL GOVERNMENT

George Washington, *Virginia, 1732-1799*
Charles Carroll, *Maryland, 1737-1832*

Benjamin Franklin, *1706-1790**
Alexander Hamilton, *1757-1804**
Roger Sherman, *Connecticut, 1721-1793*
John Hanson, *Maryland, 1715-1783*

III. STORY OF NATIONAL PIONEERING
1800-1860

1. PIONEERING IN EXPANSION

Thomas Jefferson, *1743-1826**
William King, *Maine, 1768-1852*
John Sevier, *Tennessee, 1745-1815*
Thomas H. Benton, *Missouri, 1782-1852*
Marcus Whitman, *Washington, 1802-1847*
William Allen, *Ohio, 1803-1879*

2. PIONEERING IN TRAIL BLAZING

Stephen F. Austin, *Texas, 1793-1836*
Sam Houston, *Texas, 1793-1863*
Dr. John McLoughlin, *Oregon, 1784-1857*
Rev. Jason Lee, *Oregon, 1803-1845*
Marcus Whitman, *Washington, 1802-1847*
Brigham Young, *Utah, 1801-1877*

3. PIONEERING IN GOVERNMENT

Thomas H. Benton, *Missouri, 1782-1858*
Henry Clay, *Kentucky, 1777-1852*
Andrew Jackson, *Tennessee, 1767-1845*
John C. Calhoun, *South Carolina, 1782-1850*
Daniel Webster, *New Hampshire, 1782-1852*
William Allen, *Ohio, 1803-1879*
John M. Clayton, *Delaware, 1796-1856*
Jacob Collamer, *Vermont, 1792-1865*

4. PIONEERING IN SCIENCE

George Washington, *Virginia, 1732-1799*
Benjamin Franklin, *1706-1790**
Robert Fulton, *Pennsylvania, 1765-1815*
Robert R. Livingston, *New York, 1746-1813*
Dr. John Gorrie, *Florida, 1802-1855*
Dr. Ephraim McDowell, *Kentucky, 1771-1830*
Dr. Crawford W. Long, *Georgia, 1815-1878*
Sequoya, *Oklahoma, 1770-1844*

IV. STORY OF COLOSSAL STRUGGLE
1860-1875

1. Struggle for State Sovereignty
Jefferson Davis, *Mississippi, 1808-1889*
Alexander H. Stephens, *Georgia, 1812-1883*
Gen. Robert E. Lee, *Virginia, 1807-1870*
Gen. E. Kirby Smith, *Florida, 1824-1893*
Gen. Wade Hampton, *South Carolina, 1818-1902*
Gen. Joe Wheeler, *Alabama, 1836-1906*

2. Struggle for Preservation of the Union
Abraham Lincoln, *1809-1865**
Gen. Ulysses S. Grant, *1822-1885**
Gen. Lew Wallace, *Indiana, 1827-1905*
Gen. Edward D. Baker, *1811-1861**
Gen. Philip Kearny, *New Jersey, 1814-1862*
Gen. James Shields, *Illinois, 1810-1879*

3. Civilian Struggle for the Union
Francis P. Blair, *Missouri, 1821-1875*
Thomas Starr King, *California, 1824-1864*
Lewis Cass, *Michigan, 1782-1866*
Samuel J. Kirkwood, *Iowa, 1813-1894*
Hannibal Hamlin, *Maine, 1809-1891*
Oliver P. Morton, *Indiana, 1823-1877*

4. Struggle for Reunion and Peace
James A. Garfield, *Ohio, 1831-1881*
Zachariah Chandler, *Michigan, 1813-1879*
Gen. Wade Hampton, *South Carolina, 1818-1902*
Gen. Joe Wheeler, *Alabama, 1836-1906*
Zebulon B. Vance, *North Carolina, 1830-1894*
Francis H. Pierpont, *West Virginia, 1814-1899*
John E. Kenna, *West Virginia, 1848-1893*

V. STORY OF TREMENDOUS DEVELOPMENT
1875-1914

1. Western Movement Accelerated
John J. Ingalls, *Kansas, 1833-1900*
J. Sterling Morton, *Nebraska, 1832-1902*
George W. Glick, *Kansas, 1827-1911*
Henry M. Rice, *Minnesota, 1817-1894*
George L. Shoup, *Idaho, 1836-1904*
James P. Clarke, *Arkansas, 1854-1916*
William Jennings Bryan, *Nebraska, 1860-1925*

2. Cultural and Social Improvement
J. L. M. Curry, *Alabama, 1825-1903*
James Z. George, *Mississippi, 1826-1897*
Charles B. Aycock, *North Carolina, 1859-1912*
William H. H. Beadle, *South Dakota, 1838-1915*
James Harlan, *Iowa, 1820-1899*
Uriah M. Rose, *Arkansas, 1834-1913*
Frances E. Willard, *Illinois, 1839-1898*

VI. BEGINNING OF A NEW NARRATIVE
1914——

William Jennings Bryan, *Nebraska, 1860-1925*
John Campbell Greenway, *Arizona, 1872-1926*
Robert M. LaFollette, *Wisconsin, 1855-1925*
William E. Borah, *Idaho, 1865-1940*
Huey Pierce Long, *Louisiana, 1893-1935*
Will Rogers, *Oklahoma, 1879-1935*

*Statue given by United States Government.

National Statuary Hall Epitomizes the Story of America

I. BEGINNING A GREAT NARRATIVE
1607-1770

The statues of great men in the Capitol Building of the United States do epitomize the long and varied history of this Country. No modern nation has had a more remarkable development than America has had on this new continent. So vast is the continent and so varied its development that it would seem improbable that a collection of 86 persons in marble and bronze could possibly reflect the progress of the Nation from 1607 to the present time, in its sweep from the Atlantic to the Pacific. National Statuary Hall does depict that marvelous story.

Of course there was a beginning. The founding of European settlements on the new continent was that beginning, and that era has representatives in Statuary Hall. It must not be overlooked that the founding of European settlements included not only English but Spanish and French. It is a narrow view of American history to assume that it all springs from Jamestown and Plymouth Rock. While the English were at work on the Atlantic seaboard the Spanish had begun even earlier in the South and the far West, and the French were in the North. All this is portrayed in the fact that Massachusetts Bay Colony (the State of Massachusetts) sent the Puritan, John Winthrop, as one of her representatives to Statuary Hall.

Winthrop was a fitting example of the best of English culture transplanted to a "stern and rockbound coast", and he represents the Puritan religion as it shifted to America.

The Pacific coast State of California sent her earliest Spanish missionary, Junipero Serra, as one of her contributions to National Statuary Hall. It was a glorious chapter written by the Spanish padres in their service to God and King that often contrasted greatly with the Spanish military conquests, but nowhere is the colonizing zeal of the padres illustrated better than in California, and no finer example could be named than Junipero Serra who established nine missions in fifteen years.

It is also significant that the State of Wisconsin has sent the French missionary, James Marquette. While it is true that the French power was broken by the English in four Colonial wars, French influence is indelibly impressed upon the Northland, and a part of that influence was the daring exploration of such men as Father Marquette, in opening up the heart of the continent to civilization.

As a contrast in religious faith, Rhode Island has contributed her Roger Williams. Great as was the Puritanic faith of the New England founders, an element of religious liberty and individual judgment in matters of belief was badly needed, since "a little leaven leaveneth the whole lump." Roger Williams as the pride of Rhode Island furnished such leaven of religious liberty.

But the beginning of civilized life in America was not entirely a matter of European settlement. Several Colonial Wars were fought to determine which Nation should predominate, and thus the soldier had a part in these beginnings. New Hampshire sent that soldier to Statuary Hall—John Stark, the volunteer who fought nine years in the French and Indian Wars.

Thus John Stark took a part in that half century of conflict which determined that England rather than France should control North America. Later this outstanding soldier took a part in the American Revolution, which was the military phase of our struggle for independence.

II. STORY OF AMERICAN INDEPENDENCE
1770-1800

Declaring Independence

The numerous English colonies planted on the Atlantic seaboard consolidated after a due lapse of time, and formed thirteen practically self-governing colonies which rapidly grew into commonwealth status. By 1770, or within a half dozen years after the last of the French wars removed a danger from their backs, they began to know their importance and had a growing spirit of self reliance. By the decade of the 70s in that century they were able, though reluctant, to cut the apron strings of the mother country if harsh treatment drove them to do so. It did.

In the whole development toward independence which is known as "The American Revolution" there are, for our purposes four distinct movements or steps, although they may overlap somewhat in point of time. Let us call these steps: DECLARING INDEPENDENCE; FIGHTING FOR INDEPENDENCE; PREPARING FOR LOCAL SELF-GOVERNMENT; and FOUNDATIONS FOR NATIONAL GOVERNMENT. Some of these movements occurred almost simultaneously; some of the great men who carried them on figured in more than one; and our National Statuary Hall is populated by great men from each movement.

Of course, the ultimate outcome of the first movement was the famous Declaration of Independence of July 4, 1776, passed by the Continental Congress that year, but preceding it there was an anxious period of history leading up to the momentous decision. It must be remembered that not all English subjects in America were of one mind nor did they resolve in a single day to cut the political ties that bound them to England and to assume an independent political status. Much heart searching and many trials of patience and waiting occurred before the final break came on July 4, 1776.

The thirteen American colonial governments had taken an important part in the French and Indian War—the last of the four colonial wars—which determined that English rather than Frenchmen should work out the destiny of North America. Englishmen living on the shores of North America had generously contributed in men and money toward the decisive victory culminating in the Treaty of Peace of 1763. They were proud to have done so. George Washington is placed in our National Statuary Hall by Virginia partly for his role in that war as well as for other more important reasons. However, the full career of George Washington helps to epitomize the "Half Century of Conflict" between England and France in North America.

John Stark began to build up his remarkable military record before the Revolution by fighting Indians and the French in the last colonial war. He thus enabled the State of New Hampshire to send him as one of her contributions to this great assemblage in marble and bronze at the Capitol. Many colonists, like George Clinton, fought for England before the revolutionary battles of Lexington and Concord. Therefore, American subjects of England for a decade after the Treaty of 1763 felt that they had done their full patriotic duty to the Empire and had earned "their board and keep", and they were getting more and more restive under the new financial and oppressive measures of King and Parliament. This was especially true of businessmen like Samuel Adams and John Hancock of Boston, whose businesses were adversely affected by the tightening of British policy.

Accordingly, the leading men of the period took counsel together in their "Committees of Correspondence" with every tightening of the mother country controls. Such colonial leaders as Samuel Adams heartened and emboldened each other by letting the other colonial leaders know what each had done under trying circumstances.

Connecticut has very appropriately placed Roger Sherman among the immortals in this Hall. Sherman of Connecticut has the great distinction of being the only one of this illustrious band of revolutionary leaders who actually signed all four of America's first great state papers. Powerful as the sword is, he well illustrates the truism that "the pen is mightier than the sword." He signed the significant Non-importation Pact of 1774 before signing the Declaration of 1776, and before signing the Articles of Confederation of 1778, and long before signing the Constitution of 1787, which brought about "the more perfect union." We need to remember, too, that Roger Sherman was a member of the Committee that drafted the Declaration of Independence.

Samuel Adams is often called the "Father of the American Revolution." He is placed in our historic assemblage by Massachusetts, and properly so, as one whose life sums up the spirit of the Revolution. His work as an organizer of political forces, like that of Roger Sherman and like that of John Hancock, was as necessarily a part of the total revolution as was the work of generals and other military men.

The Second Continental Congress was gradually growing more determined than the First Congress had been and many of its members felt sure by early 1776 that a break with the mother country was inevitable, but by June that year several of the semi-independent governments among the Thirteen had not yet authorized their delegates at Philadelphia to take the momentous step for independence. However, in June of that year the Congress did pass this resolution: "That these United Colonies are, and of right ought to be, free and independent States, that they are absolved from all allegiance to the British Crown, and that all political connection between them and the State of Great Britain is, and ought to be, totally dissolved." Some delegates to the Continental Congress did not vote on this resolution because their governments at home had not yet authorized them to do so. Later the vote became unanimous.

Thomas Jefferson, whose marble statue at the Capitol was the gift of a grateful Nation in 1855, was among the five men chosen to draft a suitable declaration, and he did most of the composition, so that he is rightly called the author of the Declaration of Independence. However, he was later sent on a diplomatic mission and was out of the Country in 1787 when the Constitution was signed. Benjamin Franklin of Pennsylvania was also one of the five on the Committee to draft the Declaration, and as always, played a significant part there—almost as significant a part as he later played in the total revolutionary movement. Of course he was a Signer of the Declaration and later a Signer of the Constitution. National Statuary Hall boasts of eight signers of the Declaration of Independence: Samuel Adams of Massachusetts; Charles Carroll of Maryland; Benjamin Franklin of Pennsylvania; Thomas Jefferson of Virginia; Caesar Rodney of Delaware; Roger Sherman of Connecticut; and Richard Stockton of New Jersey, after John Hancock.

Fighting for Independence

We must carefully distinguish the various "steps" toward independence, and never lose sight of the equal necessity on the one hand of whole heartedly resolving for independence, and, on the other hand, successful civilian and military struggles to attain an enduring independence. When Benjamin Franklin said, "We must all hang together or assuredly we will all hang separately," he had in mind more than one phase of the hazard. The word "revolution" as used in the term, "The American Revolution" does of course include the war for independence, but it connotes also a certain amount of change in local and general civilian government for America.

If the authority of the King of England was to be repudiated; if the laws of Parliament were to be invalidated in America; and if the Royal Governors were to be expelled, then the thirteen colonies or states must assume for themselves more or less self-government, choose their own home rulers and create at once a united over-all government, at least on a temporary basis. The Continental Congress was such a temporary, over-all government. It had met in 1774, the year before the fighting had begun, hoping to avoid the impending conflict, but when the war actually started Congress at once chose George Washington, one of its Members from Virginia, as General to lead the armies of liberation.

On June 16, 1775, the Continental Congress unanimously chose Washington to take full command in the field, which he did after modestly expressing doubt as to his ability and refusing pay for his services. As stated earlier, Washington had helped to break the power of France in America for England. After the Revolutionary War had been won he helped to unite America under the Constitution of 1787. Following that date he served two terms as the first President under that Constitution. Any one of these services would have made him immortal. However, it was as a general winning the War of Independence that he deserves the greatest fame. If Virginia had not chosen him as one of her two great representatives in National Statuary Hall a grateful Nation would have placed him there. He was no mere local hero, but was and is of national and international stature. In fact, Washington is one among a score of the world's greatest men of all time.

The great commander needed the heroic service of younger men all through the war and often got it. General Nathaniel Greene of Rhode Island was one such. General Greene's brilliant conduct of the war against the British in the southern colonies was but one of the young General's military contributions toward victory. Thus Rhode Island had good reason and just cause to select him as one of her representatives in this Hall of American immortals.

Alexander Hamilton was another young aide to Washington both in war and peace, but Hamilton made a greater name for himself and later rendered greater service to the nation in matters of government than he did on the field of battle. His statue is the gift of the Nation.

Certain governors like Jonathan Trumbull of Connecticut made the success of the ragged, half-starved American army possible by their material aid along with their upholding faith. One patriotic war governor, Caesar Rodney of Delaware not only furnished supplies and men, as Trumbull of Connecticut did, but Rodney led his militia in battle. Almost the same may be said of George Clinton of New York. Of course, Connecticut and New York and Delaware would appropriately select such Revolutionary War governors as their representatives in National Statuary Hall.

It takes all kinds of men to make up an army, and General Washington had them, as for example, the fiery Ethan Allen of the Vermont frontier, and the God-fearing Christian, Muhlenberg of Pennsylvania. Both of these men called upon the Deity, each in his own way; both helped the cause of the Revolution; and both deserve to be honored as they have been by their respective states. Ethan Allen turned his boundless energy from questionable activities to patriotic service. Muhlenberg laid aside the vestment of the pulpit for the uniform of the soldier. Washington needed such men.

Foundations for Local Self-Government

Because the Revolutionary War, as a military struggle, lasted for seven years, it was necessary for Americans to have a suitable form of government while they were carrying the struggle to completion and victory. It was one thing to throw off the government of the King of England and Parliament in the middle 70s (1774-76) and quite another thing to bring about a more perfect government in the late 80s (1787-89). But what was the nature of their government during the intervening years between those dates when Americans were fighting desperately most of the time and victory hung in the balance?

Let it be clearly understood that two types of government had to be set up during those years. Local government in each of the 13 colonies had to take the place of its former colonial government. According to the independent spirit the Americans had, each colony had declared itself to be an independent State, the word State being spelled with a capital S. Then, also, in order to "hang together" effectively in the sense that Franklin meant it, the thirteen new States must form some sort of overall government as strong as the sovereign jealously of the 13 new States would permit, to save them all from the vengeance of the British Empire against which they had rebelled. Let us look at the governmental conditions during the dozen years involved.

Not all of the thirteen colonial governments were exactly alike. At the outbreak of the Revolution about half of them were "Royal Colonies" and had governors not elected by the people but appointed by the King of England as "Royal Governors." True, these colonies had what might be called elementary legislatures, but the King's word together with Acts of Parliament constituted their law and it was enforced more or less rigidly by the King's Governors. Of course, with the coming of the Revolution the Royal Governors were expelled when the King's power was repudiated and the people in those colonies had to write State constitutions and provide legislatures to make their own laws. In royal colonies the people built home government from the ground up in a truly revolutionary way.

Beside the royal colonies there were two other classes of colonies. Some of the thirteen colonies were "proprietary colonies" and were supposed to belong to the Lord Proprietor, such as William Penn or his heirs. In such colonies the Lord Proprietor appointed the Governor instead of the King's doing so. In the proprietary colonies the people generally had more to say about their own government than in the royal colonies. That depended upon the liberality of the Lord Proprietor.

In the third class of colonies known as "charter colonies" the people in each had been granted a charter, more or less liberal in its terms, and in these charter colonies the people for years had had considerable to say about their own affairs. Accordingly there was less, and less need for, "revolutionary change" in the "charter colonies." But each colony had to have, or sadly needed to have, some outstanding man or men to shape up their local government to make it suitable for the prolonged struggle for ultimate freedom.

It is not surprising that subsequently most of the "Old Thirteen" original States sent the best of such early founders to the National Statuary Hall. That is all the more true as some of these local "State makers" also took a worthy part in the founding of the central or united government, for all the States, practically at the same time. As a further mark of distinction some of these founders of the thirteen States and the United Confederacy of States also served in the army and helped the cause with both sword and pen. Caesar Rodney of Delaware might be named to illustrate such threefold title to fame, although George Washington is a better example. If Benjamin Franklin of Pennsylvania had had a part in the military fighting he would be an example, for he took part in every other element of the struggle except the military. What did others do?

Jonathan Trumbull was placed in the Hall of History by Connecticut. What did he do? He was Governor before the King's yoke was thrown off. He defied the King and promptly helped to convert the colony into the new State of Connecticut. He was an intimate and wise adviser of General Washington and gave spirit as well as much material aid in the darkest hours of the war. Samuel Adams has been mentioned before. He should be remembered as "The Father of the American Revolution." Without carrying a gun he fought the good fight locally in Massachusetts at Boston and centrally at what was then the National Capital, Philadelphia. Samuel Adams, as well as John Adams, was sent by Massachusetts to the Continental Congress. John Hancock was also notable both at Boston in Massachusetts and at Philadelphia for Massachusetts. George Clinton and Robert R. Livingston of New York, and John Hanson of Maryland served their respective States at home in this critical period and also at Philadelphia as members of the Continental Congress.

The Continental Congress, of course, had a president each year of its existance. Why then are some Presidents of the Congress honored more than others? John Hancock was not the first President of the Congress but he was President in 1776 when the revolutionary step was taken of adopting the Declaration of Independence. That places him. The Continental Congress was a revolutionary body lacking full legality until the Articles of Confederation (the first Constitution of the United States) was adopted formally by all thirteen States, which occurred in 1781. John Hanson of Maryland was President of

111

Congress when that first Constitution became effective, and in that sense may be called the "First President of the United States of America."

George Clinton of New York, besides fighting in two wars and serving as Governor during the latter part of the Revolutionary War, also helped as a civilian in establishing self government legally and nationally for a free people. Robert R. Livingston also of New York won a niche in fame as a diplomat in purchasing Louisiana and also in sponsoring steam navigation which helped to bind our vast country together and to make *E Pluribus Unum* a physical reality.

Foundations for National Government

As has been said earlier, the rebellious American colonists, on announcing their independence from the Mother Country, had to fight for it, and at the same time had to set up some kind of over-all government to enable them to bring their united strength to bear on gaining freedom, and also at the same time to set up self-government within the 13 new States which they declared to be free and independent. This took wise and courageous leaders and fortunately each colony had them. We cannot name them all but are particularly interested in those worthy men who were afterward selected by their respective States to be placed in National Statuary Hall.

These English colonies had been settled from 1607 to 1732, and the lapse of time up to 1774 had enabled all of them to gain some maturity. For that reason when they rebelled against King and Parliament it was the idea that each should thereby become an independent, self governing State. But they knew that not one of the thirteen States alone could stand against the British Empire. In union was their only hope, and so began their long efforts toward a suitable union. At first the efforts were weak and the results unsatisfactory. Years had to elapse before America attained that "more perfect union" which enabled her to write *E Pluribus Unum* across her history and across her broad areas.

If in the beginning the States were thirteen independent governments, the first meeting of men to represent all of them would, in the nature of things, be a meeting of diplomats, or "a Congress," as the words then implied, instead of a meeting of lawmakers, or "Parliament," as the lawmaking body in England was called. The first general meeting of these early American "diplomats" met at Philadelphia in 1774 and was called the First Continental Congress. There was at that time no captial city officially named and no constitution to provide for all this. Philadelphia was centrally located and was then our largest city and had a commodious "state house" and other convenient quarters for their meeting. This first Congress started the move for separation by discussions which braced all to back up those colonies like Massachusetts who had taken the lead in the direction of rebellion and independence.

The Second Continental Congress met again in 1775 and finding that the war had actually started at Boston, resolved to see it through and support Massachusetts. They appointed George Washington as General of the combined forces. All recognized that this Congress was a revolutionary body and that it must continue to meet and to advise the thirteen States and also lead the country to victory. It did several acts preliminary to the Declaration of Independence the next year. Let it be remembered that the Continental Congress had very select men from the States. Two should be named because they each served as "President" of the Congress at critical times in history. John Hancock was President of the Second Continental Congress at the time when the Declaration was adopted on July 4, 1776. As President it was his duty, pleasure and honor to sign the Declaration first. Because his business in Boston had suffered from recent action of the British government, he was more than usually anxious to declare independence, although he knew well that if the attempt failed it would mean his execution. John Hancock was bold and signed his name in bold letters, so, as he said, King George III could read it without specks. Another John, John Hanson, was President in 1781 when the Articles of Confederation became effective.

The Articles of Confederation had been

planned as early as 1776 since a committee to draft the document had been named at the same time that the committee of five was named to draft the Declaration of Independence. The Articles were intended to give America, when approved, the United States of America. In spite of the urgency for union to win the war, the thirteen States were jealous of each other and reluctant to form a strong government over all. Washington and the American army suffered greatly from this lack of efficient, united support. It was five years before the States accepted this first constitution, weak as it was. By 1781 The Articles of Confederation became the law of the land, and it was then that John Hanson of Maryland was able to signify the approval of Maryland, which was the 13th and last State to give formal ratification.

The Articles of Confederation did not bind the States together very well, even in the desperate years of war. When war ended there was even less adhesion. For awhile after 1783, after the treaty which gave the thirteen States their complete independence, it looked as though America was destined to have on its eastern seaboard 13 jealous, quarreling, fighting nations which might repeat on this continent the bloody history of Europe. The States were tending to pull apart from each other. Someone called the Articles of Confederation "a rope of sand." Wise statesmen were trying to save America from the fate of such disunion.

The convention that accomplished the great object of giving America "a more perfect union" was the Constitutional Convention which met at Philadelphia in the spring of 1787, and drafted the present Constitution of the United States. This was the most memorable meeting in American history. The present Constitution, without its later amendments, was completed in about four months and was signed by 39 of the members in Old Independence Hall at Philadelphia, September 17, 1787. General George Washington had presided over this notable convention as chairman or president. Naturally he signed it first—G. Washington. Besides Washington, the men who signed the Constitution and were afterwards honored by their respective States by being placed in our National Statuary Hall were: Charles Carroll of Maryland; Benjamin Franklin of Pennsylvania; Alexander Hamilton of New York; and Roger Sherman of Connecticut.

Not all of the men named were conspicuous in the constructive work of the Convention, other than in signing the finished document, but they were helpful and effective in their respective States in getting it adopted by their State conventions called to act upon it. Alexander Hamilton did his greatest service in connection with the Constitution by getting the key State of New York to adopt it, and Hamilton's influence extended in a subtle way toward its adoption in other states.

Charles Carroll and Roger Sherman had great influence in their states as did Franklin in Pennsylvania. However, no man in Statuary Hall had a greater part in shaping the Constitution than did Benjamin Franklin, and none in the Convention equaled him unless it was James Madison of Virginia, who has been called "The Father of the Constitution." This alone would entitle Madison to a place in Statuary Hall, had there not been a limit of only two from each state. Benjamin Franklin did many other important things to earn him the great honor. He, too, would probably have been chosen by Massachusetts, the state of his nativity, or by Pennsylvania, the state of his adoption if his statue had not already been placed in the Capitol by the Government before National Statuary Hall was created.

III. STORY OF NATIONAL PIONEERING
1800-1860

Pioneering in Expansion

Kings and emperors in olden times used to measure the success of a reign by the extent of the enlargement of their domains. Well, that is one measuring rod, even though it is not the best. During any given period of early American history the growth of our nation might be gaged by the extent of territorial expansion. Since our expansion has not been

113

altogether or even largely by conquest; and since we have not taken over well inhabited, civilized lands from neighboring nations who needed those lands for immediate expansion; and since our nation has not deprived any nation of its place in the sun, our territorial growth is not properly subject to censure as in so many other instances in history. Our American territorial expansion is not entirely free from criticism of world opinion but very largely so. Therefore, our expansion in lands —although not the only or best gage of growth—is one properly to be noted.

The most notable thing in America's growth and development has been the western movement. That means first of all, occupying new lands to the West. Those great Americans who properly obtained for our people those vast lands to the West deserve a place in the "Hall of Fame" for that if for nothing else. The English King in 1763 drew a line down the Eastern (Alleghany) Mountains and forbade his loving subjects to cross it going West. But Daniel Boone and many like him never heard of that decree and would not have obeyed it if they had. So that Royal attempt failed to "fence in" that generation of Americans on the Atlantic seaboard. Fortunately, the able American diplomats, including Franklin, in making out the Treaty of Peace of 1783, were able to fix the back border, or western boundary, in the middle of the continent at the Mississippi River. This was not due to English generosity, because American arms during the War had taken possession that far west. In fact, the original thirteen States on the Atlantic coast, on becoming one nation, had plenty of room out West in which to grow for a long period without buying or conquering any more for many years. Significantly, the original United States of America (the old thirteen States) in effect became on this continent "The Mother Country" to many political children, or new States formed to the West. In fact the original United States of America became a great colonizing power and settled this new continent under a far better colonial policy than the mother country, England, had shown in her early colonialism.

The first big chunk of territory added to our national domain was Louisiana, purchased by President Jefferson through a great diplomat who is also a figure in our Statuary Hall, Robert R. Livingston of New York. The purchase of Louisiana alone would have made Thomas Jefferson or Robert Livingston immortal in American history and yet that was only one of a half dozen very important acts of Jefferson and regarded by him as less important than the three for which he wanted to be remembered and had indicated on his grave stone. Jefferson was a philosopher — especially a political philosopher — but he did not scorn material wealth, such as an abundance of free land, knowing full well how political freedom is favorably conditioned by a high degree of economic freedom, which plenty of free land, that may be had for the taking, engenders in a people.

The settling of our open land was not a complete, thorough-going straight line movement due west. There was some sparsely occupied land lying north of New England toward the St. Lawrence River, claimed by Massachusetts, including the area of Maine, but the title to which was not made clear by the Treaty of 1783. There were several flaws of title to "Maine" which needed to be straightened out. The settling and building of the State of Maine was aided politically, industrially and in other ways by William King who became its first Governor when Maine was admitted in pair with the State of Missouri in 1820. Maine sent William King to Statuary Hall.

Before the rushing tide of migration jumped the Mississippi River into the farther West, there was considerable "mopping up" to be done on the wilderness, by way of settling it, between the eastern mountains and the Mississippi. Daniel Boone had broken a path through a natural mountain gateway—the Cumberland Gap—and thus bent two widely separated westward moving streams of migrants into the region of Tennessee. That fact seemed to predict that the Tennessee area should contain the first new State formed west of the mountains. It did. It was largely the work of John Sevier and was called the "State of Franklin." John Sevier is in our National Statuary Hall sent logically by Tennessee.

Under the head, PIONEERING IN EXPANSION, we should extend the narrative to the Pacific Ocean, north and south, which would bring in the story of Dr. John McLoughlin, Stephen F. Austin, Sam Houston and Brigham Young at this point. However, these four are reserved for a different kind of pioneering. Thomas Hart Benton of Missouri, Marcus Whitman of Washington and William Allen of Ohio will next be considered as they are responsible for sending the flag to the Pacific Ocean. This is due in part to their official work in Washington in shaping the policy of territorial expansion.

Thomas Hart Benton was United States Senator from the new, key State of Missouri from the date of its admission in 1820 to 1850. He saw a lot of American history in his *Thirty Years View* and had a big hand in making it. Thomas H. Benton really made Missouri "The Mother of the West" by his encouragement from St. Louis of the profitable fur trade and by his fostering from Independence (Kansas City) of the "Commerce of the Prairies" between the States and the Spanish and Mexican inhabitants of Santa Fe and other northern outposts of Spanish settlements. It is not surprising then, that Missourians carried the Flag following the two types of commerce over the Santa Fe Trail into the Spanish realm. Certainly Missouri should put Thomas Hart Benton into National Statuary Hall. And Missouri did just that.

Marcus Whitman first called attention to the Pacific Northwest as a prized region about to be lost and thus aroused an indifferent nation to save it from going by default to another nation. No wonder the State of Washington has sent Marcus Whitman to this famous collection of great Americans. But although the American Flag was advanced to the Pacific both in the far Southwest and the far Northwest, it took the great expansionist, William Allen of Ohio to uphold the hand of the Democratic Administration of President James K. Polk, and to see to it that the acquisition—by purchase, by treaty or even by risk of war—added the three vast domains: Greater Texas; Greater California; and Greater Oregon, to the National limits. If Ohio had not sent William Allen to National Statuary Hall because of his part in that expansion, the Nation should have done so.

Pioneering in Trail Blazing

Having just noted the official work of seven great Americans regarded by their respective States as worthy of being signally honored for the part they played in extending our National boundaries, let us turn now to six other occupants of National Statuary Hall for their contribution of a somewhat similar nature. These six, less officially and more privately than the others, made the widening of our national boundaries significant and effective by blazing trails into the little known western regions either before or after those regions became our territorial possessions. The six are: Stephen F. Austin of Texas; Sam Houston of Texas; John McLoughlin of Oregon; Reverend Jason Lee of Oregon; Marcus Whitman of Washington; and Brigham Young of Utah. These men went in person into the new lands, sometimes at their own expense, to conquer and to occupy them, whereas most of the preceding list played a political role in acquiring additional lands or firming national control of them. America has been a nation of trail blazers, but millions like Daniel Boone, have gone on an individual basis instead of heading movements such as these six men have led.

Stephen F. Austin in carrying out his father's dream of settling an Anglo-American colony in the Texas area of the Republic of Mexico, went out from Missouri to Texas to establish his colony beyond the borders of his own nation and in accordance to a contract under Mexican Law. The Austins were not the only Anglo-Americans who cast longing eyes upon lands belonging to Mexico, but the Austins were conscientious, honorable men, intending to be law-abiding citizens of the government of Mexico. It turned out another way, and these self-exiled Americans before long had to fight another war for independence, which they won. In winning the War of Texan Independence the groundwork was laid for Texas to become a part of the United States of America.

Sam Houston was the most outstanding among the many notable men who went from "The States" into Texas to help Texas win her independence from Mexico. Houston became the first President of the "Lone Star Republic," and being well and favorably known by statesmen at Washington, he worked with others to bring about the admission of the Texan Republic as a State in the American Union, after ten years with an independent existence. All this is one big reason why Texas honors Sam Houston in National Statuary Hall.

Strange to say, Dr. John McLaughlin, whom the State of Oregon sent to Statuary Hall, unlike Austin and Houston, was not originally an American citizen and did not become so until very late in his life. His great contribution for which he is now honored was made while he was a citizen of another nation and while engaged in business which was competitive with Americans. He was sent into the far West to the Oregon Country—which included then a large area on either side of the Columbia River—by the Hudson Bay Company to hold and exploit the fur trade and such natural resources of that country for Canada and England. However, he welcomed the American missionaries, especially the Reverend Jason Lee, and helped them make homes in that new land. Rev. Lee and Marcus Whitman were "Soldiers of the Cross" who established Protestant Christianity in the Columbia area and brought the elements of civilization which are the necessary foundations of American States.

Brigham Young was another trail-blazer who went outside the boundary of his own country to make a new home for his people in the western mountains and deserts. It so happened that soon after Brigham Young made his settlement in the Great Salt Lake area, the American Flag waved over that region as a result of the successful conclusion of the War with Mexico and a provision of purchase. President Young was the second great leader of this new religious group officially known as the Church of Jesus Christ of Latter Day Saints, but commonly called Mormons, and because of serious differences with neighbors in several States back East, he sought to take his people to a land so uninviting that none would want to take it away from them. Brigham Young himself led his people West to found a Christian commonwealth which he called the State of Deseret, which he later hoped to get admitted as a State along side of California. This failed but many years later Deseret was carved up into several States and the core of it was admitted as the State of Utah. Then Utah sent Brigham Young, a magnificent statue of marble to the National Statuary Hall in Washington.

Pioneering in Government

The first six decades of the 19th Century in the United States witnessed a vigorous peacetime growth of our nation, as the American people built new States in the West and shaped their institutions to meet local needs while keeping all within the framework of the great Constitution of 1787. Each new State toward the West became both a springboard and a pattern for yet newer States farther West, all attracting overflow populations and spreading improved American ideas of democratic society and local self-government. These Western States also had their leading statesmen who would later be suitable candidates for any "hall of fame." To illustrate, Missouri had her Thomas Hart Benton, just as Kentucky had her Henry Clay and Tennessee had her Andrew Jackson.

Mention of Andrew Jackson reminds us of John C. Calhoun, Daniel Webster and several others in the older eastern States who pioneered in ideas of government for the entire nation during this middle period. All of these leading men of that time gave deep thought to a correct interpretation of the basic Constitution of 1787, and at the same time sought proper law and policy for the entire nation under that Constitution. Andrew Jackson favored a liberal public land policy for the settling of the West, but Daniel Webster was not enthusiastic about offering free land in the West to entice people to migrate from New England. Andrew Jackson inclined toward a loose money policy, largely under local control and free from monopoly, for the benefit of the common people. Webster favored the Hamiltonian policy of finance with its centralized banking and a "sounder" stabilized currency. When Jackson became President he killed the United States Bank and thus won his point—temporarily.

While Calhoun, Clay and Webster fought desperately in the United States Senate over constitutional interpretations, Benton of Missouri looked to the far West, even to the Pacific for new regions into which Americans should carry the Constitution and the Flag. If our national boundaries were to be rounded out at that time to the far Pacific and our commerce extended to that ocean, we should have not only overland connections as Benton envisioned but seaway connections as John M. Clayton of Delaware foresaw. Clayton gave the State of Delaware many reasons for sending him to Statuary Hall, one of them being that as a diplomat he paved the way for interoceanic commerce across the Isthmus of Panama by negotiating with England the Clayton-Bulwer Treaty.

The great constitutional debate, lasting for a generation over the nature of this union of States, was led on the one side by John C. Calhoun of South Carolina aided by Alexander H. Stephens of Georgia. This school held that this union is a confederation into which the sovereign States came voluntarily and peacefully for their own good, and from which union each sovereign State might secede, or withdraw peacefully and legally if its best interests seemed to require. The opposite school was led by Daniel Webster of Massachusets who held that this Union "is an indestructible Union of indestructible States." (Webster's statue was sent by New Hampshire).

Meanwhile political and judicial views and opinions were being evolved and advanced by the statesmen of that generation, as the maturing government grew and strengthened. Already our National domain was vast and much of it sparsely settled, thus raising two other great questions causing much debate between opposing schools of political thought. How much territory does Uncle Sam want or need? And what kind of men, slave or free, should occupy those lands? William Allen of Ohio was with the "Manifest Destiny" school, envisioning limitless expansion on this continent. Jacob Collamer of Vermont, and other New England Whigs thought that America's West should be the home of free men, and shaped their political and judicial views toward "Free Soil and Free Men." It took bloodshed to end these great debates.

Pioneering in Science

Such men as Robert Fulton of Pennsylvania, Ephraim McDowell of Kentucky, and John Gorrie of Florida, and others sent to Statuary Hall by their respective States as a signal honor, were not outstanding soldiers or statesmen. They were honored for quite a different reason and yet they merited that honor the same as the soldier-statesmen who stand beside them.

America has astonished the world as a nation of inventors and scientists, and has written a record of progress in the natural sciences as appealing to the mind of man throughout the world as is her record in the political realm, and in the whole field of statecraft. For instance, the name, Edison, any place on earth, makes people think of things made and done according to divine and natural law, just as the name, Jefferson, any place on earth, recalls the principles of governing mankind in justice and equity according to the laws of God and human nature. Although the two great fields of science and statecraft are quite distinct and separate, some notable Americans occupied both. It is nothing to Edison's discredit to say that American inventiveness did not begin with him. Franklin and Jefferson were scientists and inventors before him.

Many theories have been advanced as to why Americans are a nation of inventors, no one cause being considered the only one. Our people have much natural ingenuity when put to the test. "Necessity is the mother of invention." Coming to subjugate a new land rich in natural endowment but not too easily tamed, Americans have continuously had their ingenuity taxed to the uttermost to conquer this great continent. Labor was re-

117

quired, and naturally labor-saving devices were sought. Distances were great and travel necessary, so travel conveniences were called for. Life in rural America far away from the comforts and amenities of cities called for inventions with a social meaning. Raw nature may be beautiful or rough or cruel. It took sturdy settlers to conquer new regions and many settlers died young. Progress in medicine and surgery was desperately needed, and it was provided, as the roll of National Statuary Hall testifies.

Science is a very broad term as applied to human life and service. In a way George Washington, as a Virginia farmer, may be said to be one of the earliest Americans to evolve scientific agriculture. He saw that the wasteful tillage of his day needed to be corrected, and he did it both by precept and practice. Washington was not the only founding father who took time off from statesmanship to improve man's well-being. Benjamin Franklin gave his country and the world many useful inventions from his own hand and brain, and Robert Livingston gave much needed encouragement to Robert Fulton in the invention of the steamboat. The debt which the country and the world owe to Fulton and Livingston for the epoch-making steam transportation cannot be estimated.

There are social inventions, difficult to measure, but every whit as useful to man as any mechanical or physical invention. The unschooled Cherokee Indian, Sequoya, set his people on the road of progress by his invention of the Cherokee alphabet, by which the Cherokees came to have a written language. They had newspapers, books and schools ahead of most other Indians.

Dr. Ephraim McDowell of Kentucky did marvelous things in surgery through his own skill and daring and encouraged that profession for saving human life. He was the first surgeon in the world to cut into the abdominal cavity and remove an ovarian tumor. And that in 1809—the year Abraham Lincoln was born, and 33 years before the first use of sulphuric ether as an anesthetic in surgery. It was Dr. Crawford Long of Georgia who first used ether in surgical operation, in 1842, and thus saved humanity untold suffering through the proper use of anesthetics. Dr. John Gorrie of Florida in attempting to minimize suffering in sick rooms in warm countries, invented the ice-making machine. Think of the outgrowth of his mechanical refrigeration. Suffering humanity and normal humanity owe an unestimated debt to those three humanitarians for their gifts to the nation and to the race, and all who pass this way are obligated to the States of Kentucky, Georgia, and Florida for recalling this service to us and honoring those men in National Statuary Hall.

IV. STORY OF COLOSSAL STRUGGLE
(1860-1875)

Struggle for State Sovereignty

The great struggle which cost the Nation so much in wealth and blood a century ago and which furnished so many candidates for eternal fame from both sides of the Mason and Dixon Line was our War Between the States (1861-1865). The impending conflict had disturbed the public mind for a generation before 1861, and its multiplied results engrossed the best minds for a generation after 1865. More than a fourth of all men in National Statuary Hall had some connection with one or more of its phases.

Since it "takes two to make a fight," and there were two sides to this struggle, the candidates for fame may be listed on each side separately, beginning with the Southern Confederacy—though without attempting to show who caused the War. The causes of the war were both immediate and remote, apparent and also deep. However, the first shot was fired at Fort Sumpter.

It must be understood that this terrible conflict raged over two conflicting constitutional theories concerning the nature of this union of States. The leaders of the South held that the central government was but a convenient union of sovereign States and that the powers of the United States were limited and only such as the sovereign States had delegated to it for their own protection and benefit. The States were sovereign, they said, and Southern constitutional lawyers led by Alexander H. Stephens of Georgia and John C. Calhoun of South Carolina evolved several related ideas of action out of the Doctrine of State Sovereignty.

Two notable ideas growing out of the Doctrine of State Sovereignty were the Doctrine of Nullification and the Doctrine of Secession. By nullification was meant the power and legal right by State legislative action to nullify, or make of no effect, any act of the government at Washington to which any sovereign State objected or thought it should be nullified. By secession was meant the legal and constitutional right of a sovereign State to secede, or withdraw, from the Union, without treason or war, when it felt conditions warranted such a move. If the doctrines of nullification and secession are correct constitutional law, then the Acts of Congress depend upon approval of State Legislatures for their validity and the union of the United States remains intact only until some sovereign State resolves to pull out and go its separate way. Many prominent Southern leaders, such as Stephens and Calhoun, held these views. Alexander H. Stephens was the deep student of the matter, and John C. Calhoun was the man of action in legislative halls.

On the other hand, Daniel Webster and many other leaders in Northern States held that the United States of America was a sovereign state with a higher sovereignty than any component State, and that the Union is "an indestructible Union of indestructible States." Many like Webster thought that American liberty had been obtained only through union and only through perpetual union could perpetual liberty be held. Webster exclaimed: "Liberty and Union, now and forever, one and inseparable." And thus the issue was drawn.

Abraham Lincoln, of course, held the Websterian view so strongly that as President he never admitted that the Confederate States had ever gotten out of the Union, even though the Southern States formally passed Resolutions of Secession. As President he attempted to enforce the laws of the United States over those Southern States by force of arms. This meant war.

The States of the deep South resolved on secession, formed a loose union of themselves known as the Confederate States of America and fought to gain their independence from the government at Washington, somewhat as the original thirteen colonies had done from the English King in the Revolution. The Confederate States of America had a Constitution which compares remarkably with the Constitution of 1787 for the United States of America. Most of the former was copied from the latter—which latter, of course, is our Constitution today — but their points of differences are revealing.

The Confederate States of America chose Jefferson Davis of Mississippi as President, Alexander H. Stephens of Georgia as Vice President, and Robert E. Lee of Virginia as General in command of their armies. These three men are proudly placed in our American Valhalla, National Statuary Hall, by their respective States, together with a half dozen other fighting men of the South—General E. Kirby Smith of Florida; General Wade Hampton of South Carolina; General Zebulon B. Vance of North Carolina; General Joe Wheeler of Alabama; General James Z. George of Mississippi; and Colonel J. L. M. Curry of Alabama. All of these men fought desperately for what was to be a "Lost Cause," each giving his highest allegiance to his Sovereign State, but after defeat each returned to give devoted service to the Flag of the United States of America and "to the Republic for which it stands."

Struggle for the Preservation of the Union

It has been said rather thoughtlessly that the election of Abraham Lincoln in 1860 caused the War Between the States, but the verdict of history seems to be that this War would have come to America if Lincoln had never been born. Lincoln's election in 1860, under the attending circumstances, might have "triggered the explosion," but, even so, it could have been only a minor cause. Historians often make two classifications of causes of great historical events — major causes and minor causes, and have done so for this American tragedy. The major causes of the Civil War are several and they lie deep and run far back in America's past.

If Southern leaders had read President Lincoln's First Inaugural Address before moving to secede they might not have taken that step at all. Near the end of that address on March 4, 1861, Lincoln said this:

" In your hands, my dissatisfied countrymen, and not in mine, is the momentous issue of Civil War. The government will not assail you. You can have no conflict without being yourselves the aggressors. You have no oath registered in Heaven to destroy the government, while I shall have the most solemn one to 'preserve, protect and defend' it."

And dreadful war came!

One of Maine's contributions to our National Statuary Hall, Hannibal Hamlin, was Lincoln's Vice President during the four years of the Civil War. The War President also had good civil advisors in his strong but sometimes stubborn Cabinet. He did listen to all, and then determined his own action as Commander-in-Chief. Of course, he needed and finally got able generals although he had to make numerous adjustments before he got the best.

The two fighting teams may be contrasted in several respects, only one of which will be mentioned here: President Abraham Lincoln of the United States of America had to try out and make several changes in top notch field commanders before he brought General Ulysses S. Grant to the central theater of war in Virginia. On the other hand President Jefferson Davis of the Confederate States of America had one top grade field commander in General Robert E. Lee all during the War. The two military experts were pitted against each other between the rival Capitals, Washington and Richmond in the Virginia theater of war—until Appomattox.

Both military chieftains, Grant and Lee, had able subordinates as generals in command of armies, some of which generals on the Southern side, as we have seen, have had their statues presented by their States to our National Statuary Hall. Of the generals on the Northern side who have been thus honored we may mention here: General Lew Wallace of Indiana; General Philip Kearny of New Jersey; General James Shields of Illinois; and General Edward D. Baker who left the Halls of Congress to die on the battlefield and whose statue has been presented by Congress for the Nation. There are others who were high ranking military commanders in Northern armies whose statues have been sent to Statuary Hall and whose military careers entitle them to such honors but who had other great achievements to their honor. They will be mentioned in another connection.

The spectacular and tragic death on the field of battle of General Kearny and General Baker certainly merit a Nation's grateful memory.

The case of General Lew Wallace, a Union commander at Shiloh, also merits special mention. The Battle of Shiloh was said to be the bloodiest battle in the West and the second bloodiest battle of the War. The struggle of the Union forces to take the Mississippi River to the Gulf was vital and desperate, and General Wallace had plenty of stern matters to attend to which he did—quite well. However, even during this campaign he could not forget his writings. It is said he often wrote at night in a tent by the light of a lantern. If that be true, General Lew Wallace is perhaps one of few men of pen and sword who could pass so readily and quickly from highest fiction to sternest reality on the bloody banks of the Tennessee River in mid-western America.

A philosopher at one time said, "Battles are but ideas hitting their hard heads together." Many hard battles between Fort Sumpter and Appomattox over ideas concerning the nature of this American Union of States finally determined what both Abraham Lincoln and Daniel Webster thought—that this is "an indestructible Union of indestructible States," and thus the Union was preserved.

Civilian Struggle for the Union

When the tragic conflict of Civil War began to seem inevitable, and the war clouds had begun to darken for a decade or so before the outbreak, patriotic men in both sections tried hard in every honorable way to avoid it. It appeared to be an irreconcilable conflict which no concessions or compromises seemed able to prevent. The great triumvirate in the Senate — Calhoun, Clay and Webster — had passed from the land of the living about a decade before fighting started, and their leadership was greatly missed. But it is doubtful whether, if living, any one of them could have done much further to prevent it.

Henry Clay from the Border State of Kentucky had always exerted a moderating influence. He became known in American political history as the Great Pacificator because of the rather effective compromises he helped to bring about in 1820, in 1833, in 1850, and throughout the years in controversial legislation affecting the rival sections, North and South. But Henry Clay died in 1852, Daniel Webster later that same year, and John C. Calhoun had preceded them—so there were new pilots at the helm of the Ship of State.

The poet, John Greenleaf Whittier, a cousin of Webster, and a one time great admirer of his distinguished relative, the Senator, was bitterly disappointed with one of Senator Webster's efforts in 1850, an effort at compromise to avoid a break and inevitable war. Whittier wrote a short but scathing poem entitled, "Ichabod," about Webster, very expressive of the tense feeling building up in the country. Now, when the gentle Quaker Poet, Whittier, could write such a poem as "Ichabod" about a reasonable American statesman, relative or no relative, it shows the hot feeling prevailing between North and South. The Country sadly missed Webster the next ten years, and Whittier missed him, too, and mellowed toward him as time passed, and expressed that kindlier feeling in the poem, "The Lost Occasion."

Francis P. Blair's statue was contributed by the State of Missouri, and a world of history justifies the honor. Blair is credited with saving the border state of Missouri to the Union, and that one feature may have turned the tide of war against the Confederacy. Blair did some actual fighting but his greatest efforts were of a civilian and political nature. As a 100% Democrat he broke with the Southern Democrats and went all out for the preservation of the Union and against secession. Years later, when peace had returned and was assured, Francis P. Blair returned to the Democratic Party to serve his State and Nation.

Abraham Lincoln belongs not alone to Illinois but to the Nation because of his contribution. As President and Commander-in-Chief of the armed forces he played his greatest part in the military struggle to preserve the Union, but he made a notable effort as a civilian toward that end. Not the recipient of much formal education, Lincoln's great mind was a storehouse of American political history. His knowledge of Constitutional law was remarkable and his ability to state great problems in the language of common people was unmatched. He begged for moderation rather than war. His plea to the Southerners in closing the First Inaugural Address is one of the finest appeals in the English language:

"I am loath to close. We are not enemies but friends. We must not be enemies. Though passion may have strained, it must not break, our bonds of affection. The mystic chords of memory, stretching from every battlefield and patriot grave to every living heart and hearthstone all over this broad land, will yet swell the chorus of the Union when again touched, as surely they will be, by the better angels of our nature."

Just prior to the outbreak of war while the doubtful border states were trembling in the balance deciding which way to go, several men played a decisive part in their respective states as did Blair in the State of Missouri when he did the seemingly impossible by keeping that "key" State from going with her Southern sisters. Thomas Starr King did much the same thing for California. California was in a sense a "border state," too, and there were indications that she might go with the South. The Southerners made great efforts to tie her to the Confederacy. Those efforts failed largely because a Unitarian Minister lately come to California from New England preached powerfully all over that big State, loyalty to the Union and the Flag.

Jacob Collamer of Vermont, Lewis Cass of Michigan, Hannibal Hamlin of Maine, and

Samuel J. Kirkwood of Iowa either worked in their civilian capacity to try to prevent the outbreak of civil war, or after the outbreak they helped powerfully as War Governors or high civil officers to win the war and preserve the Union. Kirkwood of Iowa is a good example in that he threw the weight of the Governor's Office into the struggle on the side of the Union. Governor Kirkwood financed more than Iowa's part of the war and furnished an over-quota of volunteers so that the draft law was not needed in the State of Iowa during the war.

Struggle for Reunion and Peace

The history of the War Between the States contains the names of many generals and that is reflected in Statuary Hall, which is natural enough for such a momentous struggle, and generals are apt to be conspicuous for a generation after such a war. Generals have much to say about the conduct of a great war and sometimes about the terms of peace even in America where the Civilian Head is Commander-in-Chief. Fortunately, in this case a victorious general, Ulysses S. Grant, had something to say about the immediate terms of peace. No defeated general in the history of war was ever accorded more kindly consideration than General Robert E. Lee received from General Grant to whom General Lee surrendered at Appomattox. Unfortunately the civilian rulers of the victorious government were less inclined to forgive and forget and put away animosities than were President Lincoln and General Grant.

President Lincoln's tragic death just at the moment of victory for the Union arms boded ill for the conquered people. What to do with the Southern leaders, both civilian and military leaders, was the question. Lincoln's small son asked the President, "Father, what will you do with them? Hang them?" And President Lincoln is said to have replied, "Yes. Hang on to them." Such a reply was in keeping with Lincoln's political philosophy—that there was no possibility for a state to get out of this Union. It was also in keeping with his great heart to hold on to the erring sister States and the erring fellow statesmen and their people. All too few of the civilian leaders in the North agreed with President Lincoln and his proposed "general amnesty" for the Southern people, and a harsh program was adopted toward them after Lincoln's death which program lasted for a decade following the surrender of Lee.

The period of reconstruction was filled with bitterness. Wisely, it seems, the extremists of this period in the North were not chosen for National Statuary Hall. And the surviving leaders of the South who were chosen for the Hall were chastened men, and men whose renewed loyalty to "The Old Flag" dedicated them to the great task of healing the wounds of war and laying the best foundations for peace. Fortunately, and wisely, nearly all the men of the Reconstruction Period in the North who were fit candidates for Statuary Hall favored reunion of North and South and a constructive peace, and they, too, labored with rededicated Southerners to that end. This spirit of cooperation, which finally won over vindictiveness, was of great significance to our future.

The Lincoln-Johnson Plan, or Presidential Plan of Reconstruction, was moderate and sensible and if carried through fully would have healed the wounds of war quicker and would have saved much bitterness. Lincoln's death and Andrew Johnson's ineptness prevented fulfilment of that Plan; therefore a modified Plan changing from the President's idea of dealing with the South was put through by certain leaders in Congress. This is often called the Congressional Plan of Reconstruction. It was much more severe on the Southern States than the President had planned. However, the important thing to note is that despite delay and bitterness the real leaders on both sides of the Mason and Dixon Line worked together to minimize the terrible losses, to save the fragments and to build for peace and prosperity.

From this disturbed reconstruction period the South later sent to Statuary Hall such men as Governor Zebulon B. Vance of North Carolina, General Wade Hampton of South Carolina, and General Joe Wheeler of Alabama, all of whom had fought hard in war, had been defeated and then fought the battles of peace for their States and Nation. Governor Vance served in Congress both before and after he was Governor of North Carolina, and it was the considered judgment of the President of the United States Senate, where last Vance served, that Zebulon Baird Vance served both his State and his Nation with patriotism and unsullied integrity.

Governor Wade Hampton of South Carolina was truly representative of the Old South, and thus increased the respect of his people for him as governor during the trying days of reconstruction, but he served the New South equally well both at home and at Washington. General Joe Wheeler of Alabama, with an unmatched battle record, was also a soldier of peace. It was said of him, "His chief public contribution was his untiring advocacy of reconciliation between North and South." Appointed major general of volunteers by President McKinley, General Wheeler left the Halls of Congress to don the U. S. Uniform in his old age and fight in Cuba in the Spanish-American War.

From the North in this period we have James A. Garfield of Ohio, Zachariah Chandler of Michigan and F. H. Pierpont of West Virginia. As America's second martyred President, James A. Garfield is assured lasting fame for that fact alone, but that is not all. His was a typical career of a man to become President in the last century. Born in a log cabin, brought up in poverty, self educated and used to hard work, he climbed the political ladder by dint of solid worth. Before becoming President of the United States, Garfield served 18 years in Congress and also received appointment to other high positions of honor and trust which he filled with dignity.

Zachariah Chandler was a typical product of New England furnished to the frontier of Michigan. In business he succeeded by initiative, honesty and hard work. At first a Whig in politics, he helped to form the Republican Party and always remained high in its councils.

Francis H. Pierpont did a very unique thing politically. He divided the great State of Virginia and carved off a portion west of the mountains large enough to make another State — West Virginia — and did it "legally" without firing a gun in doing it or being guilty of treason. This new State of West Virginia was also well nurtured in its youth by John E. Kenna whom it honored.

V. STORY OF TREMENDOUS DEVELOPMENT
1875-1914

Western Movement Accelerated

After the destruction of Civil War and the upheaval of Reconstruction had passed, reunited America resumed her onward march of progress, much changed in dominant political thinking. Gone were the opposing schools of constitutionalism headed by John C. Calhoun and Daniel Webster. The great issue had been decided. Gone was the question whether new States in the West located south of "Thirty-six, Thirty" should be slave States, and those north of that line should be free States. The Thirteenth Amendment answered that question. They must all be free States. New questions took the place of the old pre-war controversies.

Even the momentary look which the American people gave the outside world during the critical war period, occasioned by the interference of the powerful European countries —England, France, and Russia—in our family quarrel, was soon almost forgotten as the nation turned its thought inward toward economic development and westward expansion. There were questions of a different kind to be answered. Shall we give the Great American Desert back to the Indians? Shall we tame the desert as well as the Indians, and plant a lot of new States west of the Great Bend of the Missouri River? The answer to the second question meant building railroads across the Great Plains and the Rocky Mountains, damming the streams and turning water from the rivers to the parched lands to make the desert bloom under irrigation, and tapping the mineral resources of the mountains for our industrial expansion. Of course, this answer was the only correct answer.

It certainly is the only correct answer according to the notables of that period from those States in our National Statuary Hall—such men as John J. Ingalls of Kansas; George W. Glick of Kansas; William Jennings Bryan of Nebraska; J. Sterling Morton of Nebraska; Henry M. Rice of Minnesota; George L. Shoup of Idaho; and James P. Clarke of Arkansas. These men are a few examples of a generation of Western State builders who did the less dramatic and more prosaic work of establishing a half dozen states on the high plains and in the intermountain region of our great West.

But was it undramatic? Not when viewed in all its phases, for there are no more thrilling stories than some of the chapters of this history, such as the building of the railroads, the conversion of the ranges of the buffalo into grazing empires for cattle and sheep, the development of thousands of mines of the precious metals and more necessary baser metals, the conversion of burning deserts into highly productive farm lands through irrigation, and weaving all these into homes for civilized society set down in the wilderness.

Senator John James Ingalls of Kansas went to the Kansas-Nebraska area in the midst of the "Border Strife" and was thus in on that prelude to the Civil War and just in time to help lay the constitutional foundations of that new State. Governor George Washington Glick of Kansas also reached this troubled region about the same time and helped to prepare the Constitution of the new State. Governor Glick, although a Democrat, was repeatedly elected to high office in a predominantly Republican state. Both great Kansans were interested in agriculture and Glick helped to start a great continental railroad.

Having mentioned the two representatives from Kansas chiseled in marble, let us list together the two in bronze from Nebraska—William Jennings Bryan and J. Sterling Morton. Both of these bronze statues presented by the State of Nebraska are the work of the same artist and were unveiled at the Capitol on the same day. Both of these famous men from Nebraska served in Cabinet positions at Washington—Morton under President Cleveland, and Bryan under President Wilson, Morton being the older of the two. But each has other honors to his fame. Morton planted trees on the treeless plains, and founded Arbor Day, which alone entitles him to immortality in history. Bryan's fame extends far beyond the borders of Nebraska, nationally and internationally, as will be mentioned in another connection. But it was as the Voice of the West, the "Silver-tongued Orator of the Platte," the "Great Commoner" who tried to save the farmers, the laborers and all the toiling masses from being crucified on a "Cross of Gold," that William Jennings Bryan is best remembered.

It will be remembered that Henry M. Rice of Minnesota helped set the foundations of that commonwealth in the heart of the continent at the point of the beginnings of this great inland empire. George L. Shoup of Idaho performed about the same service for Idaho that Rice did for Minnesota. Both were great builders in turn as the American Star of Empire moved toward the West.

Senator James P. Clarke of Arkansas served in the opening years of this century in the U. S. Senate and, like Robert M. LaFollette, he was a champion of the people against monopoly and vested interests. While Arkansas in his day was not a highly industrialized State, Senator Clarke took advanced ground on labor and on other phases of economic legislation. Original pioneering being past, he dared courageously in a new field of social pioneering.

Cultural and Social Improvement

The turbulent years following the Civil War, known as the Reconstruction Period, lasted about a decade and were concerned mainly with political matters which had been thrown out of adjustment by the great upheaval. But political reconstruction was not all that was needed. The devastation of war had been unbelievable; the changes made by it tremendous. Construction anew on a drastically changed basis of society was called for. Poverty gripped a formerly rich land. A proud and aristocratic people could no longer command the labor of slaves but must work with their own hands. The slave had become a free man, being free to starve if unable to live in a competitive society into which he was plunged without much preparation.

Philanthropy for a generation following the fratricidal war devoted its efforts to healing the wounds of war in many ways, but especially in remedying the results of the war by helping the freedmen prepare to live as free men. Much more than emancipation proclamations, or even vitally necessary constitutional amendments were needed to aid the former slaves in their new status. The "law" as amended could and should and did protect the helpless humanity formerly held in slavery, but the new "spirit" of the nation, expressed so generously by philanthropy, made alive a hope displacing despair in these ex-slaves. Generous men donated large sums, and other noble men administered those trust funds to give a hand in lifting up the new citizens of color. The Thirteenth Amendment abolished chattel slavery, and the Fourteenth Amendment made the former slave a citizen for his own protection and that of society—which was well and good—but in addition, education was required and sympathetic social uplift both by local law and by outside generosity.

The State of Alabama has contributed the statue of J. L. M. Curry to National Statuary Hall, not because of his war record — which was outstanding — but because of his later peace record. As Trustee of the George Peabody Trust Fund he gave the South a great uplift. Mr. Peabody said, on giving his millions: "This I give to the suffering South for the good of the whole country." In that spirit the Fund was administered by J. L. M. Curry and others. Justice James Z. George of Mississippi, and Governor Charles Brantley Aycock of North Carolina, like College President J. L. M. Curry, gave their deep and serious consideration to the cause of general education in the South and threw the powerful support of their high positions, whether Chief Justice, College President, or Governor, into this cause. All three of these southern officials saw the need of education for poor whites and blacks alike at public expense, aided by trust funds generously given in the North. Governor Aycock died while attending an educational convention in a neighboring southern state.

How well did these public spirited men do their work? Twenty-five years after the War, in speaking of Negro education at home, a southern leader could say in Boston: "What people, penniless, illiterate, have done so well? For every Afro-American agitator stirring the strife in which he alone prospers, I can show you a thousand negro families, happy in their cabin homes, tilling their own land by day and at night taking from the lips of their children the helpful message their State sends them from the schoolhouse door. And the schoolhouse itself bears testimony."

Up North there was also great interest and effort on general education. James Harlan of Iowa after serving his State in the United States Senate returned home to be President of Iowa Wesleyan University, and thus he aided higher education in that progressive State. William H. H. Beadle of South Dakota was likewise concerned with the education of all citizens. As Superintendent of Public Instruction he worked for maximum benefits from public school lands. "Through his leadership twenty million acres of school lands were saved for posterity in South Dakota, North Dakota, Montana, Washington, Idaho, and Wyoming." This endowment of education with public land, which has been called "The Gift Magnificent," had its beginnings early in the first states admitted, but it was greatly increased and made significant in the newer Western States.

The State of Arkansas sent the marble statue of Uriah M. Rose to this "Hall of Fame" though he had never accepted high political office. This is rather unusual but indicates that election to the highest office in the gift of the people is but one key to distinction in America. Mr. Rose had no outstanding military or business career, nor was he a notable inventor, but he did rise to heights in his profession which was the Law. He was a scholar and a writer on constitutional law and was an outstanding credit to his profession.

Frances E. Willard is the only woman to

date honored by a place in Statuary Hall. She is thus honored by the State of Illinois. Miss Willard did her greatest work in founding the Woman's Christian Temperance Union, but she was also active in higher education for women, in woman suffrage and in related fields. Hers was a distinct contribution toward needed reform and toward placing women in their equal and rightful place in modern democratic society. The following words of Miss Willard are carved upon the base of her statue: "Ah, it is women who have given the costliest hostages to fortune. Out into the battle of life they have sent their best beloved with fearful odds against them. Oh, by the dangers they have dared; by the hours of patient watching over beds where helpless children lay by the incense of ten thousand prayers wafted from their gentle lips to heaven I charge you give them power to protect along life's treacherous highway those whom they have so loved."

VI. BEGINNING A NEW NARRATIVE
1914 ——

Great as the unfolding of the American Story has been from the first settlement down to 1914 as summarized by the lives of honored citizens now represented in National Statuary Hall, there is a distinct break in the great narrative which has justified the beginning of a new narrative after 1914. At the present we have only a half dozen men, in marble and bronze contributed by the States, who were chiefly connected with this new beginning. This part of the new narrative occupying four decades of the 20th Century is concerned with international affairs and with increasingly important domestic problems.

Prior to the World War beginning in 1914, America had been so engrossed with her own domestic affairs—growing and developing—that she had paid little heed to the rest of the world. Separated from the Old World by two vast oceans which the fleets of Britain, our Mother Country, patrolled for peaceful commerce for her own benefit but indirectly for our benefit, our young Republic grew great in her splendidly safe isolationism. Most Americans during this long period of peace did not think of the rest of the world. America grew to maturity with a minimum of international responsibilties and distractions. In a way this was fortunate for our unhampered development, but not so fortunate if we be suddenly thrust upon the stage of world rivalries to confront the hard facts of international life with little experience in diplomacy or discipline in handling international affairs. That is really what happened. Of course, America got her first idea that there is an outside world through her war with Spain at the close of the century, but in reality few Americans looked beyond our borders until the First World War engulfed us and opened for us a hazardous door.

William Jennings Bryan is the gift of the State of Nebraska to our Hall of History. He has been mentioned before in another connection because of his struggle for the "common man", his agrarian and financial policies and his campaigns for the Presidency. Now we bring him in again in this different, new period as President Wilson's Secretary of State, and Bryan's worthy but apparently futile efforts toward peace. Bryan was a great Secretary of State but did not last long. He was such a man of peace that he balked at sending stern notes to Germany which he felt might plunge us into war, so he resigned. His great achievement, which in his lifetime seemed futile, was a notable effort to negotiate peace treaties with many nations.

The World War was won by the Allies largely with American aid—men, money, shipping and munitions. One metal very vital in that war was copper, and most of it produced in America came from the State of Arizona. Arizona had just become a State and was the youngest in the Nation. An outstanding industrial engineer and mining man was Colonel John Campbell Greenway who was placed in the Hall by Arizona. Colonel Greenway, like Colonel Bryan, had fought in the Spanish-American War, and thus connects with the preceding period. However, it was his highly successful efforts in opening up new copper mines in Arizona and furnishing such sinews of war through the very modern methods of "strip mining" rather than a military career that brought him this honor. Greenway typifies on a higher level and in a newer realm the efficient, unspectacular industrial engineer who assembles capital and power machinery to win hard battles in industrial production on the deserts and in the mountains.

The marvelous development in wealth-producing power which characterizes the most recent period of the American Story astonished and entranced the world, but with the increase of wealth through the application of science came deepening poverty for many Americans, accompanied by the most perplexing economic and social problems. If Senator Robert M. LaFollette of Wisconsin, whose statue was presented to National Statuary Hall by that State, had asked himself the question, "Is this the best of all possible worlds," we know his answer from his actions, even without hearing a word. He was a prophet of Progressivism in government and an unconquerable foe of monopoly and economic privilege. Senator LaFollette helped put the State of Wisconsin in the forefront of the movement to expand the concept of democracy and to improve the governmental machinery for its operation. Wisconsin honored LaFollette, and LaFollette honored Wisconsin.

The great enigma of modern America—increasing wealth accompanied by deepening poverty—which had been noticed far north along the Canadian border in Wisconsin by Robert M. LaFollette, was also noticed in every other State. This was especially true far south on the Gulf of Mexico in the State of Louisiana. Numerous plans, some sane but many fantastic, to solve the economic riddle were proposed in the peacetime period between World War I and World War II. A plan to share the wealth and thus solve the fateful riddle appealed to a dynamic young man with brilliant mind in Louisiana—Huey Pierce Long—and sent him on the road to fame and death. Having been elected to the United States Senate from Louisiana this dedicated young Senator used his powerful position in that great forum to attract and startle the world. Senator Long was a splendid orator and he had a keen, analytical mind which enabled him as a Senator to probe the depth for information and to use the facilities of the United States government to reach the American people. While yet young he was struck down by an assassin in the midst of his work and the State chose him as one of her quota in National Statuary Hall.

This generation of Americans has witnessed a hundred times as much scientific advancement as that seen in any equal time before in any land. When we think of the movie industry and the aviation industry we are choosing two important samples, but only samples of the sum total of modern scientific progress in this country. Out of many marvels these two would probably have been mentioned by Will Rogers, the cowboy humorist, if we had asked him what two modern inventions would have astonished his ancestors who met the Mayflower, if they could have seen these things. Will Rogers became famous through the movies, entertaining millions of his countrymen. Flying was more of a recreation than an occupation with him, but he flew around the world and glimpsed tying all nations together with innumerable wings. Oklahoma appropriately honors Will Rogers in National Statuary Hall.

Idaho proudly presents Senator William E. Borah. Although Idaho is a State small in population and located in the midst of this vast continent far from the sea, this intermountain State illustrates in the influence of its distinguished son, Senator Borah, the constitutional equality of the States. In the United States Senate, even in foreign affairs, Idaho equals New York. William E. Borah spent 33 years in the United States Senate prior to World War II. His voice was heard and his influence felt not only at home but far beyond the oceans, and noted by rulers of many lands.

Now that the roll has been called of the present membership in National Statuary Hall, what of the future as the Story of America continues? The newer States will ultimately send representatives of their great leaders and enhance the story. The West is young. If the "Past is Prologue" what must the Epic be, and what the Epilogue? It would be a rash prophet who would definitely predict. But when we remember how the older States have renewed their youth, and what a magnificent superstructure of government and society they have built on the enduring constitutional foundations of 1787 and earlier precedents, and note how this heritage has been passed on to the younger States toward the West, we are reminded again of the faith and prophecy of Congressman Morrill of Vermont, as he spoke before the House of Representatives on April 19, 1864, the day his Resolution creating National Statuary Hall passed that body:

Mr. MORRILL. Mr. Speaker, as I had the honor to introduce this proposition, I desire to occupy the attention of the House for a moment. The expansion of our country from the old thirteen to thirty-six States imposed upon us the burden as well as the privilege of building and extending a structure for the accommodation of the legislative branches of the Government and appropriate for the Capitol of the foremost Republic of the world. This work is not approaching completion.

The extension of the Capitol has added so much space to existing accommodations, that the old Hall is not required as a warehouse or for committee-rooms, and it is impossible to divide and distribute it, if it were so required, in any manner that will be satisfactory, or that will not disclose an awkward, ill-begotten, ill-born, second-handed purpose, while if it shall be left whole and unmutilated as it now is, and only decorated, as now proposed, with works of art, it will appear as imposing and perfect as though the idea sprung from the brain of the architect at the foundation of the Capitol.

Congress is the guardian of this fine old Hall, surpassing in beauty all the rooms of this vast pile, and should protect it from desecration. Its noble columns from a quarry exhausted and incapable of reproduction . . . its democratic simplicity and grandeur of style, and its wealth of association with many earnest and eloquent chapters in the history of our country, deserve perpetuity at the hands of an American Congress. It was here that many of our most distinguished men, whose fame "the world will not willingly let die," began or ended their career.

The suffrages of no State will fail to be honestly and fairly bestowed, for no local shams will be intruded where the judgment of the world is sure to be challenged, and where partisanship loses its current value. We may reasonably expect that the State contributions, without charge to the national Government, will speedily furnish here in the Capitol of the nation a collection of statuary that will reflect honor upon the illustrious dead and upon the Republic found to be neither ungrateful to its distinguished sons nor unmindful of its obligations.

Notwithstanding any imperfections in the fulfillment of Congressman Morrill's vision for National Statuary Hall, as expressed above, we believe—and undoubtedly Justin S. Morrill, who spent 12 years in the House of Representatives and 31 years in the Senate of the United States, would agree—that the glory of America today will be surpassed by the glory of America tomorrow. "There is opportunity yet to blaze paths for righteousness and humanity, for freedom and for justice."